BRIAN HARRIS
THE AUTHORISED BIOGRAPHY

BRIAN HARRIS

THE AUTHORISED BIOGRAPHY

Chris Westcott

Foreword by Brian Labone

TEMPUS

This book is dedicated to Ethel and Harold,
Brian's mum and dad, who have provided unswerving support
and encouragement throughout Brian's life.

First published 2003

Tempus Publishing Ltd
The Mill, Brimscombe Port
Stroud, Gloucestershire GL5 2QG
www.tempus-publishng.com

British Library Cataloguing in Publication Data.
A catalogue record for this book is available from the British Library.

ISBN 0 7524 2696 6

Typesetting and origination by Tempus Publishing.
Printed in Great Britain by Midway Colour Print, Wiltshire

Contents

Foreword
by Brian Labone

I am delighted to add my name to this tribute to Brian, who lived a couple of miles from me near Ormskirk in our Everton days for many years. We became great mates and I was proud to be best man at his wedding to Beryl. He remains a good friend and always will be.

I used to watch Everton as a kid and first saw Brian, who was in the Army in those days, intermittently at Goodison when Everton played the Army, which included guys like Albert Quixall and Bobby Charlton – some great players. In the early days everybody thought Brian was right-winger Jimmy Harris' brother, as they both lived over the Wirral. When he came out of the Army, Brian was instrumental in keeping Everton in Division One, as we had some dodgy spells in the late fifties. It wasn't a particularly good side at the time, when money was short before the arrival of John Moores, and only then could we afford to pay sums like £30,000 for Jimmy Gabriel and £40,000 for Alex Young. Before we had Kendall, Ball and Harvey, our half-back line for a long time was Gabriel, Labone and Harris. Jimmy was only about twenty, I was twenty-one and Brian was three or four years older, so it was a very young half-back line. Brian helped bring us on and was a calming influence, at least on the pitch, as was my predecessor at centre-half, Tommy Jones.

Brian had a very good game at Wembley in the 1966 FA Cup final against Sheffield Wednesday and I remember well Eddie Cavanagh, who has sadly since died, running onto the pitch when Everton drew back to 2-2. The policeman was trying to catch Eddie, who was shedding his clothes as he was running across the pitch. When the policeman lost his helmet Brian put it on, which shows what a character he is. He's always been a joker, a very underrated left-half, as you would call them in those days, but he was very versatile. He was initially a winger, but played in many positions, and a total of over 350 games for Everton amply demonstrate his value to the club for over a decade. He was very skilful on the ball and we used to call him 'Hooky' Harris, whether or not that was because he had bandy legs I'm not sure.

Footballers are kids really, we stay kids when we have finished, and Brian's sense of humour is legendary, as you will discover in the book! I wasn't as quick as him mentally; he was always one step ahead of me. He was a bit of a schemer, a scallywag, a compete nutter on occasions, and certainly got me in some scrapes!

Brian was a very fine player; speak to any old Evertonian and they will tell you he was very underrated. This book is over-due recognition of the major part Brian played and his contribution to a very successful Everton side in the sixties. He also enjoyed success with Cardiff City and Newport County and proved there is life after Everton Football Club. I wish Chris every success with this publication.

Preface
by Bill Kenwright

Brian Harris cost Everton Football Club a £10 signing-on fee… nothing more – that was it, ten quid! Ten of the best £1 notes ever to come out of Everton's bank account! Brian could play anywhere and, in fact, he actually did. During his eleven glorious years at Goodison Park, he played in every single position except goalkeeper – and that was only because he wasn't asked!

Although he was a subtle winger with grace and speed when he arrived at Everton from Port Sunlight, he eventually became one of the pivots of the team as a defensive wing-half – a hybrid role that he took to with absolute relish. Whether he was breaking up an opposition attack, adding a cavalier thrust to a sweeping, forward movement or simply marshalling those alongside him, Brian was invariably at the very epicentre of everything that happened on the field.

During matches – be they hugely significant or run-of-the-mill – Brian would painstakingly mark out his territory, building a ninety-minute empire which he would then jealously guard and oversee.

In an era when football and the media were beginning to awaken to the idea of genuine, working-class heroes, Brian remained Everton's unsung superstar – the jack of all trades who bucked the traditional trend by mastering most of them.

He was also as adept away from the field of play as he was upon it – as I am sure you will read in the book, he was a terrific raconteur and story-teller. Brian Harris stories are legendary at Goodison Park, and are best summed up by the fact that when Everton were one of the first teams to tour the United States, they were invited on the Ed Sullivan Show. Brian supposedly was in his element in front of millions and millions of Americans in what was the top-rated show of the day. He so endeared himself to the nation with his scouse humour, that he was asked to return for another stint - but sadly his duties on the field and back home in Liverpool prevented him from becoming our own forerunner of David Letterman and Johnny Carson!

Like everyone else who spent his formative years dreaming dreams of pulling on the famous blue shirt, I had my special, personal heroes. Brian Harris was amongst the biggest of them.

I still see Brian at Goodison several times a season on match days. He doesn't make a fuss; he doesn't seek to court those who once worshipped his every move. He is content simply to lend his support to those who've been fortunate to follow in his footsteps. He inevitably brings a smile to my face and a warm glow to my already overflowing memory bank. At the recent celebration of our magnificent 100-year record of top-flight football, Andy Gray fittingly remarked that every Everton player should consider themselves lucky to have played for such a magnificent club. I can only agree with Andy's words – but also add my own, 'Yes, Andy, you were the lucky ones – but we Evertonians were privileged to be part of what you all brought to our great club.' Brian Harris, in his own unassuming way, gave as much to that blue shirt as anyone.

And, at the end of the day, he remains a gentleman and a true Blue.

Respect, Brian!

Bill Kenwright
Deputy Chairman

Introduction

Throughout his playing career, Brian Harris assumed the Everton club motto *Nil Satis Nisi Optimum* as his own personal mantra. 'Only the best is good enough' was Brian's one-man crusade. It's one he was compelled to follow as he battled against the threat of being displaced during the reign of Johnny Carey then Harry Catterick who, with an open cheque book, signed Tony Kay. But Brian was a survivor, the only Evertonian to play through the Cliff Britton era and win major honours under Catterick, and all at the highest level in English League football.

Footballers with the fortitude of Brian remain untroubled when tributes that come their way are seemingly grudging, often prefaced with euphemistic comments like reliable, durable and industrious, rarely regarded as complimentary adjectives to bestow on a sportsman – it somehow implies a lack of subtlety. 'Mr Consistency' could be interpreted as another, but is one that Brian readily embraces to describe himself, as he set himself high standards and strove to maintain them. Speak to his playing colleagues and they are unable to recall a sub-standard performance from Brian. Likewise ask them to highlight a particular match where the well-respected Brian excelled and they are equally hard pushed – 'He played well in every game,' is the standard retort.

Brian was a winger when he made his debut for Everton in 1955. After some success he was converted to a wing-half almost by chance and his career took off. Although he was right-footed he played as a left-half and immediately felt at home in this new position. He was a stylish, skilful player whose distribution of the ball early, so as to catch the opposition unawares, became his trademark. On adopting a more defensive role, his reading of the game was supplemented with a robust tackle and, for someone who measured 5ft 8½ in tall, strength in the air. He played in every position bar goalkeeper for Everton and, although left-half was his personal favourite, made many effective appearances at full-back. His contribution to the success of the Toffeemen in the sixties was typically understated but, with the experienced half-back line of Harris, Labone and Gabriel firmly established, Brian achieved his greatest personal triumph in the 1966 FA Cup final with a hugely influential display.

Brian subsequently enjoyed a renaissance with security and maturity in the autumn of his career, thriving on the responsibilities of captain, coach and manager with enormous passion for the game. He forged a successful period at Cardiff City, where his performances were a microcosm of the Bluebirds' memorable cup campaigns in Europe. Then at Newport County Brian prolonged his playing days deep into his thirties and tasted Football League management.

Brian is a character, a natural comedian whose inveterate antics worked wonders for the greater good and morale of the dressing room. There is the ultimate comparison expressed by many of his peers with Bobby Moore, borne out of the mutual gift of vision, awareness and anticipation, directly allied to his sharpness of mind, which also enhanced Brian's lightning wit off the field. Whilst adopting a professional approach to his responsibilities, Brian was a man who never let his pursuit of sporting endeavour interfere with the myriad pleasures of life. He liked a drink – we too like players who like a drink – but seemingly only as long as it happened in black and white forty years ago. He was hardly alone amongst his peers.

There was a certain innocence and simplicity about football in the 1950s, which progressively hardened in sport during the 1960s. Brian's personality reflected in part that innocence which, coupled with his natural generosity, meant that life has not always been plain sailing for him. He has had to battle against some adversity on and off the pitch during his lifetime. His sense of humour has enabled him to survive and his roller-coaster story reflects a unique mix of football nostalgia, a strain of comedy you would expect on Merseyside, but also a poignant reminder that footballers are mere mortals, like the rest of us – enjoy!

Note on the Text
The relevant team line-up appears in the text after each major game described.

1

Young Brian Earns His Spurs
1935-1954

I was born into a working-class background on 16 May 1935 at Bebington, a small town on the Wirral. We lived on a council estate at 13 Asterfield Avenue in a terraced house, with three bedrooms, one very small. I had my first football very early as a present for my birthday and two or three regularly at Christmas from my relatives; all I ever wanted to do was play football. One of my earliest memories is going into next-door's air-raid shelter during the war when the siren went, which often lasted until the early hours of the morning. Bebington wasn't heavily bombed as it wasn't a big industrial area, but I remember seeing bombs in Town Lane on my way to school. When the war was over and everybody had settled down I was football crazy and every spare moment I would be kicking a ball about. I played out in the street and also in a local field close to our house, where I kicked the ball around with my dad. He was my biggest influence in football when I was a youngster. I went to Town Lane Infants School, which was about ten minutes away from where we lived, and my mum worked as a helper with meals etc. When I was seven I went to Higher Bebington School, then when I was twelve moved to New Chester Road School, just outside Bebington.

Brian demonstrated his early sporting prowess by winning the senior athletics prize during his last year at New Chester. Taking part in the school sports he won the 100-yard, 220-yard and 440-yard races. Brian was also triumphant in the long jump and high jump contests, and unsurprisingly was a member of the Under-16s relay team. He competed in the Wirral Council of Boys Clubs' sports championships in 1950, and obtained medals for his success in the hurdles events and throwing the cricket ball. In addition to being the leading scholar in his form and captain of his house, Brian also distinguished himself by gaining the senior mathematics award and to this day has extremely neat handwriting.

I was never one for schooling, but enjoyed kicking a ball on my way to school. I did like maths and my dad gave me a pad to encourage me to write. My mother, Ethel, and father, Harold, were both born in Warrington and when Dad was transferred to Port Sunlight, they came to live on the Wirral. He was a member of the Mens' Club for a number of years, which he enjoyed very much. I used to watch Warrington play Rugby League with my dad when we went back to visit my nanna and grandad, who still lived there. My sister Jackie was born in 1942 and went to the same schools as I did. She now lives in Bromborough, the town next to Bebington. I used to feel sorry for Jackie, as I felt she was being overshadowed by my football. When I was playing for Everton my mum and dad would watch all my games, home and away. My dad passed away in 1995 at the age of eighty-five. My mum is getting on for ninety now and still gets around.

Brian's sister Jackie speaks fondly of her brother: 'I think Brian's humour comes from my grandad on my mum's side as nobody else is like that really. He was a practical joker so perhaps some of his humour came from there. Brian was into practical jokes right from the start; I had to be on my guard all the time, especially as I was younger than him. He is very kind and generous as a person to anyone. Brian's sporting ability probably comes from his father or perhaps further back than that. I loved to watch Brian play and am very proud to have seen his success. I went to the cup final with my husband-to-be, Beryl and her father, and my parents. That was obviously the highlight for the family.'

An early holiday shot (1950).

Harold Harris joined Lever Brothers at Warrington in 1925, before being transferred to the Engraving Shop at Port Sunlight in 1933. He retired as Supervisor of the shop in 1971, and then two years later was invited to join Warrington County Grammar School as a workshop technician. He utilised his Lever experience to good effect during his three years at the school. Harold was associated with the St John Ambulance Brigade for thirty years and was also Secretary of the Lever Club Pensioners' Section. Ethel was one of the factory guides at Port Sunlight during the late 1960s and early 1970s.

The nearest I had to a football hero was Billy Liddell, as my dad started to watch Liverpool play when we moved to the Wirral. He would go in the Kop and I went in the Boys' pen, so we would meet outside afterwards. I was about twelve or thirteen at the time. It was natural that I supported Liverpool; in fact I never set foot in Goodison until I signed for them. However I didn't really like watching, I always preferred playing. Dad became interested in football when I started playing, but was a rugby man coming from Warrington, and he actually played a few games for Warrington before they moved. My dad was right behind me all the time, for instance he used to get on his pushbike and I had to run behind him for three or four miles every day. I will always remember running behind him on his bike down Town Lane, where there is a public house. I was about seventeen at the time, it was quite a nice evening, and the lads that I knew were all drinking outside the pub. I got a lot of stick from them, so when I ran past I got my own back, as I told them, 'I won't be here next week, I'm playing football in Brazil!' You can imagine their jaws dropping when I told them. I'm not sure where the Brian Harris sense of humour comes from, it's not directly from my parents. I could never be serious; it just happened that I was always joking, right from the age of about six, when my dad clipped me round the ear a few times. I left school at fifteen in 1950 to become an apprentice electrician – shocking! – at Lever Brothers in Port Sunlight, a job I held for about three years.

During the latter part of his schooldays Brian played regularly on the right wing for Higher Bebington Juniors in the Fourth Division of the Bebington Amateur League. He subsequently joined the Port Sunlight Club in the West Cheshire League, while he was employed as an apprentice. Brian represented the Liverpool County FA away to the Eire FA on Whit Monday 1951, scoring a goal in a 5-2 victory, the first time that Liverpool had ever won in Dublin. The players were described as one of the best youth elevens' ever produced by Merseyside. Brian was one of seven Wirral boys in the Cheshire team that went down 7-4 to Durham at Bishops Auckland after extra-time in the FA County Youth Championship, playing again on the right wing and scoring two penalties.

Higher Bebington FC, 1950. Brian is on the extreme left of the front row.

Ray Burrows was a contemporary of Brian at Higher Bebington – 'We played together for Wirral Schoolboys and Wirral Youth, from 1951 to 1953. We won most of the games, which is not a surprise as we had at that time Brian, Alan Favarge and Charlie Jolley, who all played for England Schoolboys, and I was an England reserve. Charlie and I then played for Liverpool in the Colts, 'B' and 'A' teams, while Alan and Brian went to Everton. Brian was outside right and put the crosses on Charlie Jolley's head. He was fleet-footed and reasonably clever, but he didn't at the time stand out from the rest of the team, which was so strong. He would laugh and joke most of the time even then, and I think the fact that he was a funny man actually helped make him successful. I like the guy very much.'

At the beginning of 1952 when I was sixteen and a half I was spotted by a scout from Liverpool, who came round to see me and my parents. I was invited to train at Liverpool twice a week with some other local players – I had to catch the boat over the Mersey to get there, then the tram to their training ground, Melwood, on Tuesdays and Thursdays. The Anfield officials promised me a game in their Colts team, which was fine by me. On a Friday two weeks after starting I received a notification card from Liverpool inviting me along to take part in a match at Mellwood the following day. But the time they gave me to report to the ground was 2.45 p.m. and didn't correspond with the kick-off time published in the local paper. I assumed I would only be playing in the second half and thought they only wanted me to come along and play for a half, so I wasn't having that. I didn't think that I could really show them what I was all about in forty-five minutes. So I decided not to turn up for the match, as I preferred to play a full game for my own side, Port Sunlight. It just seemed to me that either I should be allowed to play for the whole game, or it wasn't worth the effort.

Les Bryan, who was an Everton scout, saw me in action the week after for Port Sunlight in a Saturday match and, after the game, asked me to go along for a trial. They wanted me to play with some first-teamers and reserves on the Monday in a testimonial match for a Chester City player at Chester Football Club for forty-five minutes, which again wasn't ideal, but I thought that I'd better not pass up this opportunity because another may not come along. So my dad took me to Chester; I ended up playing the whole ninety minutes, scored twice and we won 5-1. I signed amateur forms as a part-timer for Everton the next day.

When the Liverpool scout who first spotted me found out I hadn't turned up, he rang to ask what happened. I explained the letter had 2.45 on it and that they obviously weren't that keen. He just said, 'Oh, that was a typing error, it should have been 12.45.' So, but for that typing mistake, I might have ended up at Anfield. If it hadn't been for an impulsive decision – one of several I made which affected my career in different ways – I could have spent

Port Sunlight FC, 1951. Brian is on the extreme right of the front row.

Wolverhampton Wanderers Football Club (1923) Limited

MOLINEUX GROUNDS, WOLVERHAMPTON

SEASON 1952-53

Directors:

Chairman: J. S. BAKER, Esq.

J. EVANS, Esq.   C. H. HUNTER, Esq.   J. H. MARSHALL, Esq.   A. H. OAKLEY, Esq, J.P.

Manager: STANLEY CULLIS   Secretary: JOHN T. HOWLEY

Telephone: 24053/4.   Telegrams: "Wanderers," Wolverhampton.

YOUTH INTERNATIONAL MATCH
AT
MOLINEUX GROUNDS, WOLVERHAMPTON
(Covered Accommodation for 30,000)

SATURDAY, MARCH 14th, 1953.
Kick-off 3-0 p.m.

Shirts:
White

Knickers
Blue

RIGHT

LEFT

ENGLAND

ARMOUR, D.
(Northumberland)

GOODWIN, R.   GILLOTT, P.
(East Riding)   (Sheffield and Hallamshire)
2   **3**

WILKINSON, G.   SMITH, J.   EVANS, D.
(Durham)   (Essex)   (Middlesex)
4   **5**   **6**

HARRIS, B.   PUNTER, B.   JOLLEY, C.   SYKES, N.   COOPER, L.
(Cheshire)   (Staffordshire)   (Cheshire)   (Gloucestershire)   (Staffordshire)
7   **8**   **9**   **10**   **11**

Linesman—Red Flag   Referee—   Linesman—Yellow Flag
N. H. LAKIN   F. DEARDEN   P. J. MASON
(Stafford)   (Stoke-on-Trent)   (Stafford)

W. WHITESIDE   S. CAMPBELL   H. BARR   J. HILL   R. JOHNSTON
(Co. Antrim)   (Mid. Ulster)   (Co. Antrim)   (Co. Antrim)   (Co. Antrim)
11   **10**   **9**   **8**   **7**

J. H. NAPIER   W. TODD   I. BEGGS
(Mid. Ulster)   (Co. Antrim)   (Co. Antrim)
6   **5**   **4**

D. MAIRS   O. STEWART
(North Ulster)   (Mid. Ulster)
3   **2**

R. REA
(Co. Antrim)

LEFT

RIGHT

Shirts:
Green

Knickers
White

IRELAND
THE TEAMS ARE SUBJECT TO ALTERATION

fourteen years in front of the Kop at Anfield instead of fourteen happy years at Goodison. I told Bill Shankly about it at a dinner several years later and he had a good laugh about the circumstances. He said, tongue in cheek, 'You know where I am!'

During the 1951/52 season Brian played for the Wirral County Youth side and more junior honours came his way when he was a member of the Cheshire County XI and the Liverpool County Youth side. He was also selected for the England Youth International team, playing against home and continental countries at outside right – his settled position. In the match against Scotland Youth in February 1953, Brian helped England recover from a 3-0 deficit to win 4-3. Just before half-time he nearly scored when a shot rolled across the face of the crossbar. He was retained shortly after for the international against Wales at Swansea and in March 1953 played in a 0-0 draw against Ireland in front of 15,000 at Molineux. In April 1953 Brian was selected in a group of fifteen to represent England Youth in a tournament in Belgium. Following a goalless

Above: April 1953 – England Youth team in Belgium for the annual youth tournament. Brian is in the front row, second from left.

Opposite: March 1953 – England Youth line-up against Ireland Youth at Molineux. Ireland's number 8, Jimmy Hill, became a teammate of Brian's at Everton.

An Agreement made the 14th

day of January 1954 between ~~~~ of **Goodison Park**

LIVERPOOL in the COUNTY OF **Lancaster**

the Secretary of and acting pursuant to Resolution and Authority for and on

behalf of the **EVERTON FOOTBALL CLUB CO. LTD** FOOTBALL CLUB

of **Goodison Park, Liverpool.4.** (hereinafter referred to as the Club)

of the one part and **Brian Harris**

of **13, Asterfield Avenue, Bebington, Wirral.**

in the COUNTY OF **Chester** Professional Football Player

(hereinafter referred to as the Player) of the other part **Whereby** it is agreed

as follows :—

    1. The Player hereby agrees to play in an efficient manner and to the best of his ability for the Club.

    2. The Player shall attend the Club's ground or any other place decided upon by the Club for the purposes of or in connection with his training as a Player pursuant to the instructions of the Secretary, Manager, or Trainer of the Club, or of such other person, or persons, as the Club may appoint. [This provision shall not apply if the Player is engaged by the Club at a weekly wage of less than One Pound, or at a wage per match.]

    3. The Player shall do everything necessary to get and keep himself in the best possible condition so as to render the most efficient service to the Club, and will carry out all the training and other instructions of the Club through its representative officials.

    4. The Player shall observe and be subject to all the Rules, Regulations and Bye-Laws of The Football Association, and any other Association, League, or Combination of which the Club shall be a member. And this Agreement shall be subject to any action which shall be taken by The Football Association under their Rules for the suspension or termination of the Football Season, and if any such suspension or termination shall be decided upon the payment of wages shall likewise be suspended or terminated, as the case may be.

    5. The Player shall not engage in any business or live in any place which the Directors (or Committee) of the Club may deem unsuitable.

Brian's first professional contract with Everton, dated 14 January 1954, which paid him £3 per week.

ninety minutes against Belgium, England went ahead in extra time when a fierce shot from Brian was saved by the goalkeeper, but the ball ran loose to Barnes, who scored easily, and a second goal secured the victory.

I played about eight times as an amateur for the England Youth team. When I had a pub in the 1970s about six of my Youth team caps were on display, but we had a fire and I lost all but one of them. I'd always wanted to be a professional player, but my father advised me to get a trade behind me. After a couple of years at Port Sunlight I had an ultimatum from the company that if I were to sign as a professional for Everton I would have to leave Lever Brothers, as I couldn't do two jobs at once, so I left. I still have a couple of my contracts, one when I signed as a professional (as opposed to an amateur) when I was eighteen, dated 14 January 1954, which paid me £3 per week. The other is dated 12 May 1961 and paid me £20 per week, £4 for a win and £1 for a draw, with an extra £5 when I played in the first team.

Brian enjoyed rave reviews in the Everton 'C' team, a perfect illustration being an 8-0 massacre of Tranmere 'C' when he was outstanding on the wing in an attack that carved its way through the over-run Tranmere defence. Brian progressed rapidly to the 'B' side, scoring regularly during the 1953/54 season and made his Central League debut against Bury at Goodison on 2 January 1954, finding the back of the net for the last goal in a 5-0 win.

2

Debut and Life in the First Team
1954-1959

The 1954/55 season heralded the return of Everton to the First Division after a three-year absence. On 24 November 1954 manager Cliff Britton blooded Brian in the first team for a friendly match against the Army at Goodison Park. It was an impressive debut as a strong Army side, including internationals Mel Hopkins, Mel Charles, Albert Quixall and Frank Blunstone, were defeated 3-1. The Army never recovered from a three-goal blitz in fourteen minutes of the second half. After Tommy Eglington opened the scoring, Brian headed Eglington's centre into the top far corner for the second goal. The winger also contributed to the third, a header from John Parker. Mel Charles was pushed up from defence in the final stages of the game and scored a consolation goal for the Army with a left-foot shot from a cross by Blunstone.

Brian then appeared with fellow rookies Jimmy Harris and Jimmy Tansey in another friendly on 12 March 1955 in front of 31,000 at Goodison against West German side Sodingen. Again playing on the right wing, a report somewhat critically described Brian as 'making no impression on the full-back' in the goalless draw. Everton were thwarted by 'keeper Sawitzki, who made a number of excellent saves. Later in the season Everton and Liverpool reserves attracted 8,500 to Goodison Park in a 1-1 draw, Brian being the outstanding forward on the pitch. His League debut was fast approaching, as Britton was compelled to blood local talent against a backdrop of financial constraints.

I didn't really get to know Cliff Britton that well. I would sit in team talks just listening to what he had to say, not daring to open my mouth and say a word. But he did give me my first-team debut and, like most players, I'll never forget that day. Prior to that I had a really good game for the reserves against Liverpool and thought I had a reasonable chance of breaking into the first team. Everton hadn't been playing too well, and Jimmy Harris and I both made our debuts against Burnley at Turf Moor in August 1955 on either wing. We won 1-0 and both played decent games.

Everton FC 1954-55. From left to right, back row: Dunlop and O'Neill. Third row: Rea, Meagan, Tansey, Jones, Temple. Second row: Birch, Moore, Farrell, McNamara, Gould. Front row: Donovan, Hickson, J. Harris, Fielding, B. Harris.

In early sparring Brian got the better of full-back Doug Winton and slotted a through ball to Harry Potts, whose effort was just off the mark. Inside five minutes Brian slid the ball to Jimmy Harris, who passed it through the middle when he heard a call from Potts. As Potts drove into the box Les Shannon brought him down and the referee pointed to the spot. Tommy Jones coolly drove the ball into the net, sending Colin McDonald the wrong way. After withstanding early pressure in the second half, Everton almost scored a second when Brian cut into the middle to gather a through ball and glided it to his left to the unmarked Tommy Eglington. Eglington attempted to place it just inside the far post, but the ball swerved inches the wrong side. Then from an Eglington free-kick for a foul on Jimmy Harris, Brian dived in with a header which McDonald saved.

Brian's debut match was, according to the *Liverpool Echo,* Jimmy O'Neill's finest hour, saving sensationally from Brian Pilkington twice and, taking full advantage of Burnley's hesitancy to shoot, bravely diving at the feet of oncoming forwards and coming away with the ball every time. As well as describing O'Neill's performance as 'one of the greatest exhibitions of goalkeeping ever seen, right out of the Ted Sagar-Elisha Scott library,' the *Echo* covered other positive aspects of the game – 'The two debutants showed excellent control, alertness and an interchange of positions which had even

Burnley's experienced defence on one foot. What a master move it was to bring in Harry Potts between the two young debutants. He encouraged them, helped them, almost instructed them, and they responded well. The brain of Potts kept the Everton line working smoothly…I want to congratulate Everton for further proof about the policy of football production. The process of infiltration of the youngsters may be slow, but it obviously takes place, and every man at the club knows that as youth challenges so must he produce that little bit more to retain his position.'

O'Neill; Moore, Tansey; Farrell, Jones, Lello; B. Harris, Potts, J. Harris, Fielding Eglington.

This was the third game of the season and the first points of the campaign for the Blues. Brian subsequently played against West Brom and Luton before it was deemed wise to allow him to gain further experience for a month in the Central League instead of trying to rush him too early.

My first goal for Everton was against Birmingham City on Boxing Day 1955. We lost 6-2 away, then beat them 5-1 at Goodison the day after. I guess we weren't in brilliant shape on Boxing Day!

The festive spirit was conspicuously absent in the away fixture as a first-half hat-trick from Noel Kinsey saw off Everton. Brian, deputising for the injured Tony McNamara, found the net with a 'speculative drive'. In the Goodison return match Brian gave an 'impressive display at right wing, showing good footballing sense.' His performances were all the more commendable as he was only able to train as a part-timer on Tuesday and Thursday evenings. Brian was holding down the right-wing position admirably and improving with every game. He made a favourable impression in the 2-2 draw at Luton on New Year's Eve and laid on John Parker's goal, the other being scored by Jimmy Harris.

After the Luton match, Tommy Jones wrote in his newspaper column in the *Liverpool Echo*,

'Brian has made himself one of the lads over the festivities and has proved himself no mean hand at the piano. On our trip to Luton from London on Saturday morning, we stopped for lunch at a small hotel at St Albans. During the last few minutes before commencing our journey Brian showed his ability by his renderings of popular melodies. This get-together put the lads in fine fettle for the remainder of the journey. On the field Brian realised that goals do not come so easy at times. In the first few minutes, when running in for a cross from namesake Jimmy, he was just too impetuous to take full advantage of the opening. He is willing to learn and I am pretty certain should the same opportunity arise again, the result will be a goal.'

On 7 January 1956 Brian made his FA Cup debut in a third-round tie at Bristol City, who were dispatched 3-1, courtesy of goals from Eglington, Jimmy Harris and Eddie Wainwright. Brian then played at White Hart Lane on 21 January 1956 in a 1-1 draw, Wainwright again being on the score-sheet. Among those present was England manager Walter Winterbottom, who commented, 'Everton played the sort of football which has been our ideal and which will put an end to the threat of decline.' The merit of their performance was such that Everton were described as playing like a team of Hungarians on Wembley's pitch, the difference being that White Hart Lane was a couple of inches deep in greasy mud. On the wing Brian must have caused the Winterbottom eyebrows to lift in astonishment that a part-time player could show such artistry in first-class company, particularly in the second half. Brian impressed with his sureness, pace and distribution, despite the conditions.

I was called into the England 'B' squad after the Tottenham game, but unfortunately had to withdraw because of injury and Alan A'Court took my place. He won his first England cap in 1957 and I often wonder what might have been. In those days you didn't get too many chances to play for England, and if you didn't grab the opportunity with both hands, you were forgotten. I suppose that's what happened to me and I was never selected again.

I recall my first trip to London for that Spurs game. We travelled down by train from Lime Street – we didn't have the luxury coaches used by clubs these days. Not knowing about protocol I turned up at the station and got into the first carriage I saw with empty seats – except that there were a few of the big names from the team at the time already sitting there, like Peter Farrell, who I really looked up to. I shouldn't have been there at all, but by the time I'd realised my error the train had pulled out of the station – it was too late. So I sat there throughout the journey being ignored, feeling very uncomfortable, not daring to say a word in front of these top players – it was an awful trip! Having said that, as I got to know them all the senior players helped me, and I always listened to their advice. By then I had been given a nickname, 'Hooky' Harris. It came from somebody who was in the newspaper at the time, and it stuck.

By the end of that first season, Brian had made 24 first-team appearances, scoring three goals. A switch of manager in March 1956, when the inexperienced Ian Buchan replaced Britton, failed to deflect the ambition of the flying winger.

When Ian Buchan took over from Cliff Britton it didn't affect me, I had established myself in the team, but I didn't consider him a particularly good manager. As players we had a lot of respect for each other but, as he never played the professional game, it was difficult for him to gain the players' respect. Then I got an injury and lost my place, ending up back in the reserves, which was demoralising.

This downturn in Brian's fortunes was reflected in a meagre return of 3 first-team appearances during the 1956/57 season. It was something of an anti-climax after a hugely enjoyable club tour of America and Canada during the summer of 1956.

I had never been abroad before when we went to America. We sailed from Southampton to New York on the QE2 – what a trip that was, drinking gin and tonics and dancing on the boat. We had a wonderful time and I celebrated my twenty-first birthday in New York City. I remember Matt Woods, a big centre-half, carrying me back to the hotel that evening, he looked after me! We also played some football – some of the sides had guests playing for them,

1956 – Time for golf during training camp at Buxton. From left to right: Jimmy O'Neill, Tommy Eglington, Brian, Eric Moore and John Parker.

1956 – Brian watches a shot from Peter Farrell sail into the net past Vasco de Gama's goalkeeper Helio and defender Haraldo in a friendly match.

which strengthened their side. Mind you our fitness levels dropped slightly because of all the hospitality. While we were over there Tommy Jones and I met Sam Chedgzoy, a winger who played for Everton and England back in the 1920s. He played football in America until he was fifty.

There was a strong Irish connection in the early days at Everton, but everyone got on well. I didn't do my National Service at the normal age of eighteen, as I was considered a reservist with my apprenticeship, so didn't go into the Army until I was twenty-one at the beginning of 1957. I went to Aldershot and played against other countries for the British Army team, which included Bobby Charlton, Gerry Hitchens and Cliff Jones. When I was demobbed at the end of 1958 after my two years I shook hands with the Lieutenant Colonel, who said, 'What are you doing here, you work here, this is for National Service demob.' He thought I was a regular all this time! I was with Bobby at Aldershot when we flew out to Belgium for a football tournament – it was shortly after the Munich disaster, so it was a particularly sad time.

1956 – Brian at Winnipeg Airport.

1956 – Brian with Matt Woods in New York, where he celebrated his twenty-first birthday.

About the only disadvantage of being posted to Aldershot was the distance from Merseyside and some of the away games, although I was always released to play. An example was when we played Newcastle away in October 1957. It was a long train trip and, when I arrived at the hotel at Newcastle, I was told the team had gone to the pictures and that I was sharing a room with Dave Hickson. I went to my room, put my head down and had a sleep. Next thing I knew big Dave was banging and pushing me, he woke me up to tell me he was my room-mate – thanks Dave! I went back to sleep, but was woken up again at about 6.30 in the morning by Dave shaking me. I thought the door at the end of the bed led to another room of ours, but it actually led to the adjoining room next door. As we looked through the keyhole this well-known lady of the theatre was 'having it away' with a very well-known but considerably older actor! The next thing I knew ten other lads were in our room and Dave was letting them all have a quick gander through the keyhole. When we went down to breakfast Dave went up to the two of them and said, 'Did you have a good night last night?' The actor replied, 'Yes, all right!' Dave asked not quite innocently, 'Are you sure?'

The unorthodox pre-match preparations must have done the duo the power of good as both scored in an impressive 3-2 victory. Brian notched two in another

A practice swing from Brian at Goodison, 1956.

Two 1950s portrait shots of Brian.

excellent team performance at Bolton on Boxing Day 1957, when the Blues ran out 5-1 winners. Brian scored the second and fifth goal, the others coming from Hickson, Jimmy Harris and Jack Keeley, on his senior debut. Although Nat Lofthouse scored a consolation goal for Bolton in the dying minutes, Tommy Jones kept a tight hold on him throughout. It was Wanderers' heaviest defeat at home for two years, and also broke a run of thirteen games without a win for the Toffeemen.

Following a dramatic third-round FA Cup replay against Sunderland at Goodison in January 1958, Brian was detained in Broadgreen Hospital with a depressed fracture of the cheekbone. Brian's fortitude in playing on for nearly fifty minutes with the injury amazed Everton officials and the specialist, who examined him immediately after the match before he went into hospital. In pouring rain and on a mud-covered pitch Brian returned to the wing after touch-line treatment, and played a leading part in the last two goals, scored by Jack Keeley, his second of the match, and Dave Hickson, both in extra-time, as Everton secured a 3-1 victory. After the disappointment of the previous season, Brian had bounced back to complete thirty-three games during the campaign, scoring six goals, the most productive of his career.

He scored another brace in the last game of the season against Nottingham Forest in a 3-0 away victory. Jimmy Harris opened the scoring with a firm header and Brian notched the second after seventy-five minutes with another header direct from a corner courtesy of Wally Fielding. Fielding also had a hand in Brian's second goal in the eightieth minute of a one-sided affair. Johnny King starred at half-back – his performance was described as 'Perpetual motion, always in the thick of things.'

Johnny King was a holding midfield player when I was originally converted to left-half. Consequently I was allowed the freedom to push up. I only became a more defensive wing-half in the early sixties when combining with Jimmy Gabriel and Brian Labone.

In August 1958 Brian was playing outside right for the reserves in a Central League fixture, when left-back Jimmy Tansey was injured and wing-half John Bramwell was moved back to cover for Tansey. It was a pivotal moment in his career, as Brian slotted in at left-half and was so outstanding that he was given a run in the number 6 jersey in the first team. It was not all plain sailing for the fledgling half-back however, reflected in two spectacular defeats against

Everton FC 1958-59. From left to right, back row: Bentham, Godfrey, Dunlop, O'Neill, Thomas, Meagan. Middle row: Watson (trainer), Labone, Hickson, Bramwell, Ashworth, Tansey, Billington, Rea, Harburn, Bentham (trainer), Wright (trainer). Front row: Cooke (head trainer), O'Hara, Kirby, J. Harris, Sanders, Jones, B. Harris, Keeley, Clayton, Fielding.

London opponents. The first was a 6-1 loss at home to Arsenal in September, when Brian was fully stretched against the experience and mobility of Jimmy Bloomfield. Then a month later came a new low for the club at Tottenham, shortly before Johnny Carey was appointed manager to replace the courteous, but ineffective Buchan.

I'm happy to confess I played in the big defeat when we lost 10-4 to Spurs, it's in the record books. Tommy Jones tells the story that every time poor Albert Dunlop called for the ball, it ended up in the back of the net. It was amazing that Jimmy Harris managed to score a hat-trick in the game. We would always go down to Liverpool after training in the morning. We used to pass the barrow boys selling fruit and veg, have a laugh and a joke with them, and walk away with our arms full. After that defeat we had to walk miles to get out of their way, but Jimmy walked straight down past them. They said, 'All right, Jim, well done son.' We were all hiding!

Wing-halves Brian and Johnny King were unable to cope with the experience of Spurs' midfielders Danny Blanchflower and Tommy Harmer. It was a painful football lesson for the Blues and young Brian, but he typically bounced back to secure the left-half position as his permanent berth. He played thirty-five League games that 1958/59 season, as Everton languished in sixteenth place, clearly a period of transition with the advent of the new manager.

In early 1959 twenty-four-year-old Brian escaped injury when his car overturned and was extensively damaged in Birkenhead. Brian was driving towards home shortly after 2.00 a.m. when his Ford apparently skidded on the wet road. After demolishing a 'No Waiting' sign the car overturned. All the glasswork was shattered and strewn over the road, but Brian suffered nothing worse than a severe shaking and was able to scramble out unhurt. Petrol and oil spilled over the roadway and the Birkenhead Fire Brigade was called out – the wrecked car had to be towed away.

A little dog ran on the road, I swerved and missed it, and if you believe that, you'll believe anything! I did see a dog ahead of me and braked, the car skidded, the wheels locked and I went straight through the window. It was on a Thursday night, so I'd been down the Cavern and might have had a few bevvies, which didn't help. The police were called and were as good as gold. I think they recognised me, as I explained what had happened. I asked for a lift

Opposite: Everton v. Spurs, October 1958. Bobby Smith scores the seventh goal in the record 10-4 defeat at White Hart Lane. Albert Dunlop is the hapless 'keeper and Tommy Jones looks on.

Right: 1957 – Private Harris undertakes National Service.

home, but they declined! I took a taxi instead. Eventually Everton said we shouldn't be out after Wednesday night and put their foot down, I think Liverpool did likewise. They were brilliant times while they lasted; Liverpool was a really lively place. As players we all went out together and that generated a really good team spirit.

I remember going to the Cavern many times to watch the Beatles. I used to fancy myself as a singer in those days and said to Paul McCartney one evening, 'Paul, can you do me a favour and let me join in?' He turned round and went to have a word with John Lennon. I could see them looking at me, but they never let me do it, which was a great pity when I look back. We had great nights there with Gerry and the Pacemakers, or the Pisstakers as we used to call them, and Freddie and the Dreamers also performing. The Liverpool players were there as well, Ian St John and Ronnie Yeats. Most of the lads went on a Thursday night until it was clamped down on, you can imagine what we were like at training on the Friday!

```
                                          1 Trg Bn RASC
                                          Buller Bks,
                                          ALDERSHOT.
                                          ALD MIL 0435 Ext 53

                                          Ref:- 10003

                                          2 Dec 58

HQ Coy
               Subj:- POSTINGS NSM to TA
                      S/23361550 Pte HARRIS B. RASC

1. Under authy of CIC RASC & ACC Reods posting order No D1/5701/130/TR dated 15
Sep 58, the a/n is posted to TA at 581 Sup Coy RASC (15 Pet pln), TA Centre,
Coronation Rd, CROSBY, LIVERPOOL LANCS. and will proceed in accordance with
instructions given below and in Movement Order to be provided by Coy Comd.
He will report to the a/m TA Unit between 1000hrs and 1700hrs 30 Dec 58.
Then to home address:-

               13, Asterfield Ave,
               BEBINGTON, WIRRAL, CHESHIRE.

2. He will be briefed as to liabilities in TA and handed the att pamphlet
(WO Code 11839)

3. Coy will arrange final Med Examination with MO and fwd report together
with pers Docus not later than 1400 hrs 29 Dec 58 to Bn HQ.
```

December 1958 – Private Harris no. 23361550 demob papers.

3

Brian's Place is Challenged in Championship Year
1960-1963

At the start of the 1960/61 season Mick Meagan occupied the left-half berth but struggled to produce his best form. Brian was re-introduced and grasped the opportunity with both hands. Everton were expected to mount a strong challenge for honours after a promising first half of the campaign. New chairman, multi-millionaire John Moores, signalled his ambition and desire by financing Johnny Carey's purchase of a cluster of influential players, including Roy Vernon, Jimmy Gabriel and Alex Young, 'The Golden Vision'. It was envisaged that their strategic engineering would blend a more durable unit with much needed craft.

However a 1-0 defeat in the third round of the FA Cup at home to Sheffield United in January 1961 and five consecutive defeats in the League put Carey's position under threat. The position deteriorated in February when Everton reached the fifth round of the League Cup, only to be humbled in a 2-1 defeat at Shrewsbury. The architect of the victory was a twenty-year-old Rolls-Royce worker, Peter Dolby. Cycling from the factory in his donkey jacket and overalls he stopped behind the Everton coach and watched enviously at the superstars playing cards. Dolby walked to the match with the Shrewsbury faithful, his boots slung over his shoulder, and proceeded to score both goals.

The following evening Brian was ambushed by a teenage gang, but insisted on playing two days later at Goodison in a 1-1 draw against Chelsea with a black eye, swollen jaw and sundry bruises. He had been judging a beauty contest in New Brighton and was set upon outside the ballroom. Brian's friends found him lying dazed against the car and at home Ethel, his mother, said, 'He was in an awful state. I asked him to call the police, but he said he didn't want any fuss.'

My two friends went to get their coats and I went back to the car on my own. Five Teddy boys began making remarks about the defeat at Shrewsbury, I told

35

Left: A pre-match shot of Brian, 1959.

Below: Everton FC 1960-61. From left to right, back row: B. Harris, Parker, Dunlop, Labone, Thomson, Lill. Front row: Young, Bingham, Collins, Wignall, Vernon, J. Harris.

them they were drunk and one went for me. The other four came from behind and booted and punched me. I couldn't do much against five – my right wrist was still damaged from the previous week's match. They must have thought the judging was a fiddle, perhaps I didn't pick the one they wanted to win!

Soon after, Brian sought an interview with Johnny Carey after whispers that Everton were looking for a new left-half. He told the manager that the rumours had unsettled him and was assured that Everton did not contemplate signing a replacement. At the time he said, 'I feel happier now, but if Everton did sign a replacement I wouldn't be satisfied to stay here as a reserve.' It is well documented how Carey was sensationally sacked by Moores in April 1961 on the way back from a meeting in London. Finishing fifth in the League was no longer good enough for Everton Football Club. Brian for one was not shedding too many tears.

I don't have fond memories of Johnny Carey. He favoured the Irish contingent at the club and the two of us did not get on at all. I got a lot of bollockings from him because he wanted me to pass the ball more often. I used to do sprinting in Port Sunlight at an athletics club, so when I played football I used to run and run and, where there was space to go, went flying past defenders. Carey would not let me do it, he said it was a passing game, but I argued, 'If I go past two players, surely it's better than passing to him over there.' We were always arguing and he left me out of the side on a number of occasions. He wanted to coach as he played, i.e. pass the ball all the time, while I used to rely on pace, and he didn't seem to understand there were other attributes you could use in the game to be successful. Of course when I got older I passed the ball more often, but at that age I could do 100 yards in just under 10.5 seconds. We just didn't see eye to eye at all and I was in and out of the side. I heard the news he had been sacked after a round of golf at Brackenwood, Higher Bebington. When I came into the clubhouse I was straight up the stairs to celebrate with a few drinks and literally had to be carried home!

Three days after sacking Carey, John Moores announced the appointment of Harry Catterick as new manager. Catterick arrived from Sheffield Wednesday with an impressive track record and Brian was hopeful that a change of manager would result in a fresh opportunity to establish himself in his favoured left-half position.

In the summer of 1961 Everton embarked on another pre-season tour, this time to Canada and America. Both games were won in Montreal, one a particularly feisty affair against Montreal club Concordia. It was a noteworthy trip for Billy Bingham, who was sent off for the first time in his career inside

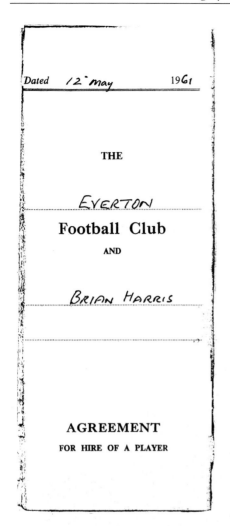

Dated *12 May* 19**61**

THE

EVERTON

Football Club

AND

BRIAN HARRIS

AGREEMENT

FOR HIRE OF A PLAYER

Left: Brian's Everton contract dated 12 May 1961, which paid him £20 per week and bonuses linked to playing in the first team and attendance figures.

Opposite: 1961 – Brian playing at Formby in the Professional Footballers' Golf Championship – he finished in second place.

twenty minutes when retaliating after being head-butted by one of the opposition. Concordia also had a player, Lopez, sent off. After all the hacking and kicking, Everton won 1-0 thanks to a goal from Alex Young. Soon after, Everton beat Kilmarnock 2-1, with two goals from Bobby Collins. A couple of weeks later Everton moved south to New York for the second stage of the tournament and a match against Brazilian opponents Bangua. Once again Bingham was sent off after losing his temper when the left-back kicked him. In many ways it was an extraordinary tour, as the following game saw Shamrock Rovers filleted 10-0. However, a listless performance from the Toffeemen resulted in a 7-2 hiding from Czech club Dukla in the first leg of the final of the International Soccer League Championship. Everton fared better in the second leg on 7 August staged again in New York, but once more were defeated, this time 2-0.

Brian's optimism for a more harmonious working relationship with the new manager was dashed on the opening day of the new season as he was dropped from the first team, Mick Meagan again taking his place at left-half. After playing every game of the New York tournament, when he looked at the team sheet on the Friday, Brian was twelfth man. He slapped in a written transfer request and at the time said, 'I'm fed up – I played in the New York tournament and all the practice games, then I was dropped.' It appeared Brian had been made the scapegoat for the two below-par team performances against Dukla.

I heard Southampton made an inquiry, but wasn't interested in going there. I didn't really want to leave Everton, it was just something I said on the spur of the moment and I eventually came off the list.

Brian had also been omitted from the last seven games of the 1960/61 season and missed the first four games of the new campaign. However, that unshakeable self-belief that characterised his play enabled Brian to fight back and regain his place, principally in the half-back line, as he completed thirty games that 1961/62 season.

Brian had been courting local girl Beryl for some time and on 11 December 1961 they were married at St Mary's Parish Church, Eastham. At the time Beryl was a dictaphone-typist for a firm of accountants in Liverpool. She has always

Everton FC, 1961-62. From left to right, standing: Labone, Parker, Dunlop, Mailey, Harris, Lill. Seated: Wignall, Bingham, Young, Collins, Vernon, Fell. Front: Gabriel, Meagan, Jones, Thomson.

BRIAN HARRIS

BOBBY COLLINS

ALEX YOUNG

BRIAN LABONE

Amusing caricatures of four Everton stars, 1961.

December 1961 – Brian's wedding to Beryl.

Brian and Beryl with Brian's sister Jackie, best man Brian Labone and Beryl's sister, Pat.

been keen on sport and was a member of the Legion Badminton Club, Little Sutton, and the Hooton and District Tennis Club. The best man was Brian Labone and the ushers were teammates George Sharples and Roy Parnell.

Brian met Beryl when he was walking his dog and Beryl was out with one of her school-friends. Brian was nineteen and Beryl, who takes up the story, about sixteen – 'I didn't know he was a footballer, I didn't know anything about football. The first time he took me to the cinema, he bought a paper, we caught the bus and he read it all the way there, he didn't even talk to me! We bumped into each other fairly regularly after that. We all used to go to the same dance hall on a Saturday at Port Sunlight village, which was built by William Lever for the employees of his soap factory. We didn't have a honeymoon as it was during the season; Brian had just the day off. He got sloshed and we ended up at Southport – we went to the cinema and Brian promptly fell asleep! He's always been a bit of a livewire; they all were at Everton, especially Labby. They socialised together in a way that doesn't seem to happen nowadays. They all went out as lads together until Everton clamped down on it. Football has always taken precedence in our marriage, it goes with the territory.'

Pre-match warm-up for Brian, 1962.

Brian continued to thrive on pitting his wits against the best talent in the country. At the start of the 1962/63 campaign John Moores stated: 'Last year I mentioned how we would like to emulate the feat of the Spurs and win the 'double', as they had just done. As things turned out, we did run Tottenham very close, finishing one point behind them in fourth position. This year we hope to go further up the League – nothing below top place will satisfy.' There was no doubting Moores' ambition to ensure the trophy sack no longer remained empty and the Blues' credentials as serious championship contenders were confirmed with an impressive victory at Old Trafford in August 1962, despite a controversial late winner.

In the last couple of minutes we broke away and Roy Vernon scored. Denis Law thought it was off-side and, as we were walking back to the centre circle, Denis was swearing at the referee. He shouted, 'You must be effing blind, ref.' It sounded really bad and the referee said, 'What's that?' Denis said, 'You're effing deaf as well!' The referee starting laughing as did everyone else and he didn't even get booked for it. I know times have changed but, if referees could be like that, perhaps there wouldn't be as many problems as there are today.

Early into the season one leading commentator noted, 'Brian is now a wing-half *par excellence*. Strong in the tackle, cultured in his use of the ball, he seems to grow in football stature with every game. He has a flair for bringing the ball through and his link-up with Roy Vernon and Bobby Collins starts many an attack. He is a bright jewel in the brilliant Everton crown of stars.' Brian's qualities had also been noted at the highest level.

Alf Ramsey always picked his strongest team and, although he would ring Harry Catterick to try and boost my confidence, I never got a full cap. There wasn't any particular season I thought I was playing at my peak. I knew I was playing consistently well right through my career and was on top of my form all the time. I remember Ray Wilson and I meeting up with some of the West Ham lads, who were staying in a Southport hotel. I came across Bobby Moore, who I used to get on well with. He thought I could get into the England team, but I said to Bobby that he was still a great player and deserved to stay there.

With the ongoing fiscal support of John Moores, Harry Catterick continued to strengthen the squad and Tony Kay was signed from Sheffield Wednesday for £55,000 in December 1962, a British record for a half-back. The Merseyside Millionaires tag was being wholly justified and ominously for Brian, Catterick promptly made Kay captain and said at the time, 'Kay was automatically on my list. I had three seasons at Wednesday as manager and rated him among the

December 1962 – Brian shields Gordon West as he foils a Tottenham attack in the 0-0 draw at White Hart Lane. Jimmy Gabriel and Mick Meagan are covering the goal and the Spurs players are Medwin, Smith, Jones and Greaves.

best wing-halves in Europe.' How ironic that Brian's sternest footballing challenge was looming on the horizon…

The day Tony Kay arrived was a very strange one for me. After training I'd gone into Liverpool city centre with Gordon West, Brian Labone and Jimmy Gabriel. There were rumours going round at the time that Tony was about to sign, so I'd gone in to see Catterick that very morning to find out what was going on. After all it was my position that was in jeopardy and I wanted to find out where I stood. Harry told me that he had no intention of signing a wing-half and totally denied that Everton were even talking to Tony. He said Alf Ramsey had been in touch about me and that, as we were in the top three in the league, he wanted to keep the same side. He convinced me that the whole story was media rubbish, so I went away believing my position was safe in the team. I was out in Liverpool that very afternoon when the Liverpool Echo *announced that Everton had actually just signed Tony Kay! I was stunned and upset to say the least. Harry had clearly known when I'd spoken to him that morning what was about to happen and couldn't even tell me. I know he had a reputation for being secretive about incoming transfers, not liking word to get out before the deal was done, but I feel he could have given me a hint, or at least not been so strong in his denial. I felt that I'd been bullshitted by my own manager and I was not very pleased to put it mildly. After the whole affair I wanted away, I felt that I'd been treated very badly and just couldn't carry on at the club. I put in a transfer request, which was accepted by the board of directors and the manager, but nothing much happened. Manchester City were said to be interested, but didn't follow it up with a firm offer, so I stayed put. I was dropped for about eight games until Mick Meagan, who was playing at full-back, was injured, so I got back into the side that way.*

Brian responded in the most effective way during a third-round FA Cup tie against Barnsley on a Tuesday evening in January 1963. It was the time of the big freeze and, facing up to the heartache that his first team days may be numbered, Brian had, 'A game they'll all remember long after I've been dropped into the reserves.' With Tony Kay watching from the stand, the pivotal moment occurred in the seventy-second minute with the score locked at 0-0. Brian collected the ball in his own half and darted like a silky skier through the centre of the pitch, with Barnsley's defence falling back on the white snow, waiting in vain for him to pass the ball. As he neared the edge of the penalty area, Roy Vernon and Alex Young made runs to the right and left, leaving him with a clear sight of goal. He made no mistake with a searing shot which ripped past the outstretched fingertips of eighteen-year-old 'keeper Alan Hill into the net via an upright. For Brian it was a magical, memorable and deeply symbolic goal and, once he had stamped his imprint on the match, the picture changed dramatically. Two more goals from Dennis Stevens on seventy-eight minutes and Vernon, who finished with a flourish on eighty-five minutes, made the fourth-round place safe.

West; Parker, Meagan; Gabriel, Labone, Harris; Bingham, Stevens, Young, Vernon, Morrissey.

Tony Kay and I didn't get on but so many years have passed, whilst you don't forget it, life is too short to bear any grudges. When we played Barnsley soon after Kay was signed I played wing-half. With the score at 0-0 I went on a run past everyone the full length of the field to score. Up to that time we were struggling, then we got another couple to win 3-0 and it gave me tremendous satisfaction.

Kay observed his new teammates qualify for a fourth-round tie with Swindon – a game he played in place, poignantly, of the man who had opened the key to the Barnsley defence. Brian made just one more first-team showing in the season, replacing Jimmy Gabriel, who had switched to centre-half because of injury to Brian Labone. As the Blues marched to their sixth championship, easing six points ahead of Spurs, there is an oft-repeated photograph of champagne flowing in the home dressing room on conclusion of the last match of the season, a 4-1 victory over Fulham. One man, who played in twenty-one League games, is missing, as the denouement of a marvellous season for the Toffeemen coincided with the most frustrating part of Brian's career.

When we won the championship at the end of that season I deliberately stayed away, I didn't want to join in the celebrations. If my place had been taken by someone I considered better than me, I would have taken my hat off to them and said fair enough, but I felt I was a better player than Tony Kay. So I had very mixed feelings when I got my championship medal. I thought I should have been an ever-present in that side and wasn't happy. I knew with my pace I was always capable of going past two or three players and creating something. I felt my best position was left-half, my favourite and preferred position, but the season after, when Kay was still playing I managed to keep my place in the team at left-back.

Everton's championship-winning squad at the start of the 1963/64 season. From left to right, back row: Rankin, Mulhearn, Harris, Labone, Heslop, McKenzie, Morrissey, Veall. Middle row: Lewin (coach), Rees, Shaw, Wright, Harvey, Thomson, Phillips, Parnell, Vernon, West, Hill, Sharples, Meagan, Young, Watson (trainer). Front row: Parker, Scott, Stevens, Gabriel, Catterick (manager), Temple, Kay, Eggleston (trainer/coach).

4

Overseas with the Toffeemen
1963-1964

The commencement of the 1963/64 season was heralded with a brief flirtation in Europe, when Everton were drawn against mighty Inter Milan in the first round of the European Cup. The first tie at Goodison captured the imagination of Blues' supporters, as a record crowd of 63,000 witnessed a predictably sterile 0-0 draw. Everton were unable to break down a typically stubborn Italian defence and managed just two chances in the entire ninety minutes. The first, early in the second half, came when Dennis Stevens headed a deep cross from Jimmy Gabriel onto the top netting of the Milan goal. Then twenty minutes from the end a header from Alex Young destined for the top corner was picked off by the agile 'keeper Sarti. In the final few minutes Inter almost snatched a priceless away goal, but Brian was on hand with a perfectly timed tackle to deny Jair, the Brazilian winger.

For the return leg in San Siro a week later Jimmy Gabriel was injured and Harry Catterick took the bold decision of giving a debut to eighteen-year-old Colin Harvey. He did not disappoint and, in a spirited performance, Everton were evicted by the only goal in the match scored by Jair, which caused great angst to Brian, who was booked during the game for his troubles. A blanket of Milanese shirts again obscured any view of goal.

I was up against Jair in both legs. We knew he was a good player, so he was marked tight in the first leg by Mick Meagan on the halfway line, and if he got loose I would have him. He shook my hand at the end of the first game and it was all very polite – I was so naive to think what a gentleman he was. In Milan I did a simple tackle on him and he started rolling all over the pitch, I couldn't believe all the gamesmanship. I remember back-pedalling towards the end of the game, encouraging Derek Temple to get closer to me. As Jair looked round for Derek I whacked him, which upset the crowd so much they were trying to get on the pitch. I think overall we were unlucky to lose, especially as the night before the game in Milan there were pneumatic drills

Portrait shot, 1963.

going on for about four hours in the middle of the night outside our hotel to keep us awake.

On the domestic scene Everton were just three points adrift of the top of the table in December 1963, but were under strength for the Arsenal game at Highbury. They trailed 5-0 after forty-seven minutes and could never camouflage a performance that was mentally rather then physically inadequate, despite Brian's best efforts – 'Harris alone could not turn back the tide, resolutely though he tried', reported the *Liverpool Echo*.

We eventually lost 6-0 and Harry Catterick put us in a lock-in afterwards to talk about the game. In our side that day was a young lad called George Sharples and when it was time for Catterick to give him some stick we all went quiet. Catterick said, 'George, I thought you were very complacent.' George replied, 'Thanks very much boss!' Then at the end of the lock-in we were asked what we thought of it all and when it came round to George he said, 'Why can't we all be friends?' No more was said!

Everton ended the season in third place, a 4-0 mauling of Manchester United at Goodison two weeks after the Arsenal game being one of the highlights for Brian, burrowing forward at left-half in the absence of the suspended Tony Kay. After neither side managed to break the deadlock in an even first half, the game opened up with one of the best-worked goals seen at Goodison for many a day. Mick Meagan carried the ball into the United half before bringing Alex Young into play. Roy Vernon then worked an opening for Derek Temple, who beat Dave Gaskell with a tremendous shot. This effort sparked off a minor goal rush and the next ten minutes saw the Blues notch another two – thanks to Vernon and Brian. Brian's goal came following a burst of acceleration through the United midfield from Dennis Stevens, playing his 350th League game. He slotted the ball to Brian, who flicked it tidily past Gaskell. United were emotionally broke and Everton completely dominant in what was arguably their best form all season, and more than adequate revenge for the impertinent 5-1 reverse at Old Trafford earlier in the season. The United goal had some narrow escapes before Stevens scored Everton's fourth with about ten minutes to play. It capped a virtuoso performance from Stevens in midfield, and his darting solo run for the last goal culminated in a left-foot shot he fired past Gaskell, which brought the house down.

Rankin; Brown, Meagan; Gabriel, Heslop, Harris; Scott, Stevens, Young, Vernon, Temple.

1964 – The Everton and Liverpool players frequently socialised. Brian is on the receiving end of some light-hearted banter at a golf meeting. From left to right: Alex Parker, Geoff Strong, Ian St John and Alex Young.

TRAVEL ITINERARY

LIVERPOOL—SYDNEY AND RETURN (26th APRIL, 1964)

	Station	Time	Via	Flight No.	Date
	Coach leaves ground	11.00 a.m.			
Leave	Liverpool	12.20 hours	CAS	526	26th April
Arrive	London	13.10 ,,			,, ,,
Leave	London	12.55* ,,	AZ	281	,, ,,
Arrive	Rome	15.10† ,.	,,		, ,,
Leave	Rome	19.45 ,,	,,	764	,, ,,
Arrive	Teheran	02.35 ,,	,,	,,	27th April
Leave	Teheran	03.45 ,,	,,	,,	,, ,,
Arrive	Bombay	09.10 ,,	,,	,,	,, ,,
Leave	Bombay	10.10 ,,	,,	,,	,, ,,
Arrive	Bangkok	15.40 ,	,,	,,	,, ,,
Leave	Bangkok	16.40 ,,	,,	,	,, ,,
Arrive	Singapore	19.10 ,,	,,	,,	,, ,,
Leave	Singapore	20.10 ,,	,,	,,	,, ,,
Arrive	Sydney	06.00 (A)	,,	,,	28th April

TOUR ARRANGEMENTS MADE BY AUSTRALIAN SOCCER FEDERATION

	Station	Time	Via	Flight No.	Date
Leave	Sydney	20.00 hours	CPA	302	30th May
Arrive	Auckland	01.50 ,,	,,	,,	31st May
Leave	Auckland	02.35 ,,	,,	,,	,, ,,
Arrive	Nandi	06.40 ,,	,,	,,	,, ,,
Leave	Nandi	07.35 ,,	,,	,,	,, ,,

BETWEEN NANDI AND HONOLULU GAIN 24 HOURS INTERNATIONAL DATE LINE

	Station	Time	Via	Flight No.	Date
Arrive	Honolulu	19.00 hours	CPA	302	30th May
Leave	Honolulu	11.00 ,,	,,	,,	31st May
Arrive	Vancouver	19.25 ,,	,,	,,	,, ,,
Leave	Vancouver	21.00 ,,	,,	,,	,, ,,
Arrive	Edmonton	22.20 ,,	,,	,,	,, ,,
Leave	Edmonton	23.05 (C)	,,	,,	,, ,,
Arrive	Amsterdam	15.25 ,,	,,	,,	1st June
Leave	Amsterdam	17.00 ,,	KLM	135	,, ,,
Arrive	London	18.00 ,,	,,	,,	,, ,,
Leave	London	19.30 ,,	STW	193	,, ,,
Arrive	Liverpool	20.50 ,,	,,	,,	,, ,,

* Flight delayed to accommodate.
† Arrival time dependant on departure from London.
(A) Optional technical landing at Darwin.
(C) Via Polar Route

Itinerary of the 1964 summer tour of Australia.

The entire football season was overshadowed by an article in the *Sunday People* on 12 April 1964, which sensationally accused Tony Kay, Peter Swan and David 'Bronco' Layne of 'throwing' a Sheffield Wednesday match. The fixture in question was a 2-0 defeat against Ipswich Town played just two weeks before Kay's transfer to Everton. They were banned from the game for life and had thrown away their careers for £100 – the betting proceeds for fixing the match. Harry Catterick was devastated but it threw Brian a lifeline, as he immediately

Brian says goodbye to his wife Beryl and children Mark and Ian before embarking on the Australia tour in 1964.

regained his number 6 shirt. It was a seminal moment in his career and there was a spring in Brian's step as the Everton squad flew out of Liverpool Airport on 26 April for a summer tour of Australia. The players were away from their wives/girlfriends and children for over a month and, as it was the first time the club had ventured so far on a football tournament, they were considered pioneers. The press lost no time in comparing some of the squad with the Beatles, especially Brian, who arrived with a Beatles haircut and soon won the heart of every Australian.

The tour started in Sydney, where New South Wales were defeated 4-1. At the beginning of May a record crowd of 18,500 saw Everton impale Queensland 5-0 in Brisbane. Barry Rees, who tragically died in a road accident less than twelve months later after moving to Brighton, scored a hat-trick. Brian waded in with the final goal. An 8-2 demolition of the Australian National side was followed by a 3-0 victory over South Australia where Gabriel, Morrissey, Gerry Humphreys and Brian all had outstanding games. A second victory (5-1) over Australia, which included ex-Toffeeman Matt Woods, was followed by a 14-1 flaying of Perth, Jimmy Hill scoring a hat-trick. Everton won all their eight games and seven were watched by record crowds. At Sydney there were nearly 52,000 spectators – and there was a rugby game played at the same time on an

The Everton line-up on tour. From left to right: Eggleston, Meagan, Harris, Morrissey, Brown, Temple, Gabriel, Scott, Stevens, Labone, Rankin, Vernon.

adjoining ground. Both Sandy Brown and Brian, whose appetite had clearly been sharpened, played in every match. 'I don't think I could have kept them off the field if I had tried,' said chief coach Tom Eggleston in the absence of Harry Catterick, who did not travel.

Australia had become more soccer-minded since the end of the Second World War, mainly due to the influx of British and European immigrants. The soccer playing fields became a common meeting place where language problems were negligible. Among immigrants were international soccer players who formed their own clubs, using their own club names. The country was gearing itself to compete in world soccer, although it took nigh on forty years for Australia to embarrass England in 2003 with a 3-1 defeat. The Australian officials were overjoyed at the way the tour went and the players were heralded as the best ambassadors for football Australia had ever had. No player since Stanley Matthews had been as popular on the field as Jimmy Gabriel, with a string of quality performances. Brian achieved celebrity status off the field and recalls some of the lighter moments.

During the tour we were invited as a team to watch a big comedian, Graham Kennedy, in Melbourne. We were all in a room by the side of the stage waiting for him to come on, when Johnny Morrissey and I decided to have a laugh. The Beatles were over there at the time and I was nicknamed Ringo. When Kennedy turned up, off we went one by one to shake hands with him. Johnny Morrissey shook hands with him and went past. I went onstage last and when it was my turn I went right past Kennedy and shook hands with Johnny, who said, 'Ringo, how are you?' I replied, 'Christ, we've got a player who looks just like you!' When the comedian said, 'No, I'm Graham Kennedy,' I answered, 'That's your fault.' Someone did say that we could do anything so we took him literally. The same evening Kennedy was doing an act in a bedroom scene, with windows at the back of the stage, rattling off jokes with another guy, when I popped my head through the window and, doing my Freddie Frinton impression, said, 'Excuse me, you haven't got a light, have you?' Two blokes about eight foot tall lifted me up and deposited me outside. That ended up in the papers and on television, as we moved on to Sydney. I used to watch Freddie Frinton on television, he always had a bent cigarette and I would mimic him. He would go, 'Excuse me,' slurring his words. I saw him appearing at a show once and he was the only person I took off.

Melbournians didn't like Sydney people and vice versa and, not having quite wrecked Kennedy's TV show, Dave Allen was doing a similar-type programme in Sydney and all his mates wanted me down on his show. Prior to meeting him, his agent said not to take the piss out of him, he was a nice guy but wouldn't appreciate it. It all went well, and Dave and I went out for a couple of pints afterwards.

Brian, the irrepressible clown, mimicked and wisecracked his way through an uproarious sequence on stage with Dave Allen, who was reduced to playing a supporting role. Allen handled the bubbly Brian adroitly and managed to avert disaster when Brian tried to recite a limerick which began, 'There was a young lady named Jill…' Allen was lucky – Brian and his teammates liked him.

Years later when I was with Cardiff City I saw in the paper Dave was appearing at a nightclub in the city, so I took Beryl there. At the interval I went to his dressing room and asked his bouncer to see him. Dave took one look at me and said, 'Bloody hell, you're following me all over the world!'

When we were in Melbourne we were invited to the Town Hall to meet the mayor. We got on the coach from the hotel and, as we were reaching the centre of Melbourne, both sides of the road were heaving with people. We were waving to them out of the window thinking we'd made it big time in Australia after only a couple of games. As we arrived at the Town Hall and got off the coach, they were all shouting, 'Where's Ringo, where's George?' What we didn't realise was that the Beatles, who had just started their Australian tour, were also invited to the civic reception and the crowds were waiting for them. We were in there for about three quarters of an hour when the Beatles arrived. I remember the mayor was wearing his huge chain of office and John Lennon got hold of it and twisted it round his neck – I don't know how it didn't throttle him!

The Everton party enjoyed a riotous farewell at the airport at the beginning of June. Proof of their popularity was the number of girls that saw them leave. The star attraction was, as usual, Beatle-mopped 'Ringo' Harris, who had led Graham Kennedy a dance on TV. Wearing his famous battered hat, a glass of brandy in one hand, a cigarette in the other and a girl on each arm, Brian had airport officials in an utter state of confusion with his antics. It was the grand finale to a tour that is still fondly recalled when the ex-players get together, forty years hence.

The trip to Australia understandably whetted Brian's appetite for life down under and there was some interest from league side Apia FC about a possible transfer, although nothing subsequently materialised. Perhaps the trip was also the catalyst for a sortie into the music world for the Everton squad, as later that year they released a single, 'Everton for me'. With his fine singing voice Brian was at the cutting edge of the record which, according to a spokesman for the record company, was ambitiously hoping to sell about 70,000 copies.

5

The Approach to the FA Cup Final
1964-1966

In September 1964 League champions Liverpool were humbled 4-0 in the Merseyside derby. In the absence of skipper Roy Vernon, Brian was made captain for the day. Everton were soon a goal up when Ron Yeats stuck out a speculative leg at a cross from Morrissey and, in a flash, Derek Temple slammed home the rebound. After thirty-five minutes, Fred Pickering manoeuvred himself into a shooting position and increased the lead with a fine low drive just inside the post. Six minutes later Colin Harvey superbly breasted down a centre to volley the ball just under the angle for the third. Johnny Morrissey completed the rout in the second half when he cut inside from the wing to lash a fine shot past Tommy Lawrence. On the few occasions that Liverpool threatened, Andy Rankin was in brilliant form and the indomitable Brian Labone completely blotted Ian St John out of the game. Demonstrating his versatility once again, Brian slotted in at right-back and nullified the presence of wide man Peter Thompson.

Rankin; Harris, Brown; Gabriel, Labone, Stevens; Scott, Harvey, Pickering, Temple, Morrissey.

I was very proud to captain Everton in that match at Anfield. Prior to the game Albert Dunlop, who had left Goodison by then, published a piece in the paper saying he knew quite a few of the Everton players were on drugs. He made a few bob out of the story, but he was only referring to when the doctor would give us a painkiller. We defended the Kop in the first half and I remember heading clear from a corner. I got there first and Ian St John caught me with his elbow under the nose. I went down, the trainer came on and gave me some smelling salts to help me come round. Of course the whole of the Kop started singing, 'Ee-Aye-Addio, Harris is on the drugs!' We were in the dressing room after the game and I said to one of the lads, 'It's terrible, I've got to go into hospital on Monday.' 'Why, what's wrong?' 'To get this smile wiped off my face!'

Everton FC, 1964-65. From left to right, back row: Morrissey, Harris, Brown, Labone, West, Rankin, Gabriel, Pickering, Harvey, Hill. Front row: Parker, Scott, Stevens, Temple, Vernon, Kay, Young, Wilson.

EVERTON HAVE IT TAPED

A new Mersey sound is on sale today in scores of record shops. It was taped in Liverpool by players of Everton's championship team. The new record is 'Everton For Me' and the players provide a chorus backing to soloist John Dunbar. Our picture shows the players at rehearsal yesterday.

October 1964 – the Blues release a record 'Everton for me'. Enjoying themselves are Jimmy Gabriel, Brian, Dennis Stevens, Alex Parker, Alex Scott, Sandy Brown and Brian Labone.

Liverpool's Thompson had good cause to remember Brian – 'He was very consistent, a super player and a hard man. I remember Brian very well as he caught me twice, but he was still a good player. Everyone talks about Tommy Smith being a hard man and a good player, but people don't say that about Brian. I've got four scars on my legs, one from Paul Reaney, one from 'Chopper' Harris, one from Norman Hunter and a scar down by my ankle where Brian caught me. They were the only players who caught me in 450 games for Liverpool.'

In November 1964 Leeds United came to Goodison for one of the most ill-tempered games in Everton's history. Referee Ken Stokes had to take both teams off the pitch in the second half to cool them down before Leeds won 1-0.

I was injured, but watched from the dugout. Leeds just came and whacked everyone in sight. That forced our lads to retaliate and Sandy Brown was sent off after only four minutes. I think the way they played was premeditated, although I'm still not sure why. In the days of Billy Bremner and Norman Hunter they wouldn't think twice about kicking you over the stand and we knew our Bobby Collins was another who would go over the top. He had size 3½ boots but they packed a hell of a punch!

Bobby was obviously a good player, but he liked to do things his way. During training at Bellefield we used to divide into two teams, with the forward line of the first team and the second-team defence playing against the first-team defence and second-team forward line. I marked Bobby and knew what his ability was, so didn't let him get a kick. I got stuck into him one time too many for his liking and after one tackle he wanted to have a fight. We squared up and the lads had to separate us, and that split us for a long time – we played together but certainly didn't socialise. Years later Beryl and I were walking along the beach on holiday in Majorca when I saw Bobby. We had a chat and it was like seeing an old friend – all had been long forgotten.

Firmly re-established in his favoured left-half slot, Brian demonstrated his drive and passion with two fine examples of his ability to break from the back. In March 1965 he scored the opening goal after twenty minutes of a 2-0 victory over Blackburn Rovers at Ewood Park. Brian and Fred Pickering linked up near the touchline and, when the centre-forward chipped the ball forward, Mick McGrath failed to cut it out and Brian was there to slot the ball coolly under 'keeper Bobby Jones. Pickering himself poached the second to make the game safe.

In evaluating Brian's career at Everton, one can't help but sense he was consistently underrated throughout his dozen campaigns. However, in

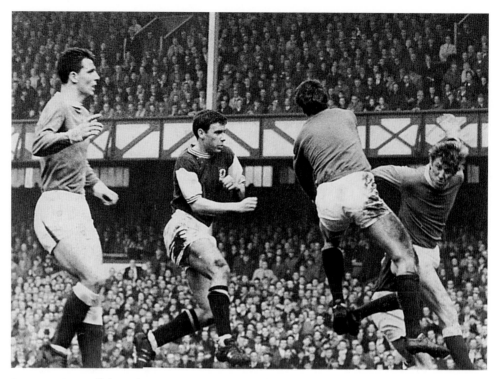

Everton v. Aston Villa, March 1965. Brian beats 'keeper Colin Withers to hit the bar with a header from a corner, with Fred Pickering looking on.

September 1965 he gave his fans something to get dewy-eyed about. When Arsenal were comprehensively outplayed 3-1, Jack Rowe in the *Liverpool Post* wrote, 'Tom Finney is always worth listening to and heeding. He was at Goodison and told me he thought Brian Harris was worth his place in the England team. There has never been a more consistent player and in this game he made a mockery of high transfer fees, because where he cost the Goodison club nothing, a man on the Arsenal side, Frank McLintock, cost £80,000 – and there was no comparison between the two. His overall play earned the maximum rating, but I cannot recall a player scoring such a brilliant goal, being foiled of another by the goalkeeper in the next minute, and thirty seconds later being laid out in the opposing goal area as he made a challenge for a centre. That was not the only time he was injured, for towards the end he was flattened by Gordon West as both sought to clear an Arsenal attack. Through it all Harris emerged as the star of the game which Everton should have won by double the margin.'

Colin Harvey's perfectly lobbed ball in the thirty-fourth minute opened the scoring for the Blues. A minute later Fred Pickering chipped to the far post, Bill McCulloch headed out and Derek Temple shot. When the ball rebounded from a defender, Temple cracked it first time into the roof of the net. One of the finest goal's in Brian's career was reserved for a minute after the interval when he started a move that found Alex Young. Brian broke through the middle for the return and, as 'keeper Jim Furnell moved, with a most delicate chip Brian glanced the ball over him from nearly thirty yards. It was a fine moment of skill and opportunism. Arsenal's consolation goal came from Joe Baker.

West; Wright, Wilson; Gabriel, Labone, Harris; Shaw, Young, Pickering, Harvey, Temple.

The Blues were promptly brought down to earth when suffering a 5-0 reverse to Liverpool in the very next match.

I played at Anfield when it was foggy and looked as though the game was being postponed. We were defending the other end from the Kop and a huge roar went up when they scored. The Kop couldn't make out the scorer so started singing, 'Ee-Aye Addio, who scored the goal?' The other end sang, 'Tony Hateley, Tony Hateley!' Back came the Kop, 'Thank you very much for the information, thank you very much etc.,' to the tune of the Scaffold song. I wasn't happy with the scoreline but had to admire the wit of the Kop.

Despite a strong showing on the home front, the Blues were unable to impress in Europe. After narrowly overcoming FC Nuremberg in the first round of the Inter-Cities Fairs Cup, a disastrous 3-0 away defeat to Ujpesti Dozsa in November 1965 left a mountain to climb for the return leg. Everton were always second best to the highly skilled Hungarian side, whose control and passing were exceptional. In front of a pitiful crowd of 4,000 sprinkled around the 75,000 Nep Stadium, Everton played defensively, with Brian slotting behind Brian Labone, but conceded an early goal after nine minutes, and two more effectively put the tie beyond their reach. Everton were undone by the arts and crafts department in the form of the deep-lying Ferenc Bene, the rising star of Hungarian football, and were ultimately given something of a football lesson.

In the return leg Everton salvaged some pride in a 2-1 victory, but were always chasing the game. For a few thrilling moments after Brian snatched a goal back in four minutes, it seemed possible that a revitalised Everton might still put their Hungarian conquerors to the test. Early spirit and enthusiasm harried the Hungarians, but an equalising goal from Lenkei after thirty-one minutes and a fine goalkeeping display from Szentmihalyi denied them. The second half was one of enormous frustration for the Blues as they were unable to break down a stubborn defence and gradually ran out of ideas. The *Liverpool Post* identified one player in particular who gave it his all – 'Everton's hero was

Brian Harris. He took it upon himself to lead the side by his example and he did it brilliantly. Never for a moment was he tied to any particular position or responsibility, except to keep driving the team on. He was in the crowded goalmouth when Ray Wilson placed his well-flighted free-kick towards the far post and an immaculate header from Harris gave the goalkeeper no chance. It was not only in attack that Harris shone, for it was a common event to see him chase two or three opponents and force them to pass. Time without number he broke up raids and must have covered more ground than any other player in the match.' A second consolation goal seven minutes from the end came when Nosko deflected Derek Temple's shot past Szentmihalyi. Brian exhibited class and spirit and, with Colin Harvey, instilled an urgency and purpose into the proceedings. It was felt that, if some of their drive could have been shifted into the forwards, there might have been a different story.

Rankin; Wright, Wilson; Harvey, Labone, Harris; Temple, Gabriel, Young, Husband, Morrissey.

My most memorable goal was against Chelsea at Goodison in February 1966. It was from well outside the box and I hit it straight into the roof of the net. It was the opening goal and we beat them 2-1.

A truly-struck ferocious drive from Brian in the first half from twenty-five yards beat Peter Bonetti just inside the post, after Alex Young had found him with a diagonal pass. Everton were jolted by a spectacularly headed goal from Barry Bridges ten minutes from the end. In the final thirty seconds Eddie McCreadie won a tackle but only succeeded in diverting the ball straight to Jimmy Gabriel at the inside-right position. Gabriel found Derek Temple who took a couple of unhindered steps before unleashing a fierce shot, which Bonetti touched onto the underside of the bar and over the line. Justice was done in an eventful, rather than great game, contested in blustery conditions. Shortly after, Brian made his 300th League appearance in the Merseyside derby at Goodison, which ended goalless.

1966 was of course a halcyon year for football, a dramatic year and a World-Cup winning year. A supreme hors d'oeuvre was served when Everton clinched the FA Cup in dramatic style against plucky Sheffield Wednesday two months ahead of the World Cup final at Wembley. Several glasses were raised that year, not least between two players in the Blues' camp.

I had a good feeling about the FA Cup run, being superstitious. The year we won the cup Everton weren't a great side and we struggled a bit in the League. We played Sunderland in the third round and were taken to

Everton v. Chelsea, February 1966. Brian celebrates his favourite goal with Fred Pickering and Tommy Wright in a 2-1 home victory.

Southport on the Friday to get all together, before returning to Goodison on the Saturday. We went to the cinema, which was about a quarter of an hour's walk from the hotel. On the way back my room-mate Jimmy Gabriel and I were at the back of the group, so we stopped at an off-licence and decided that a bottle of wine each would get us to sleep very quickly and be fresh for the next day so, with the bottle hidden in our pockets, we arrived back at the hotel. While the rest of the lads had coffee and biscuits we went to our room, locked the door and consumed several glasses of wine! We slept well and won 3-0, so superstition set in, especially as we were drawn away for the next round against Bedford, did exactly the same routine and again won 3-0. If you do something once, you have to do it again as I think it helps your confidence. Then we were drawn at home to Coventry, back to Southport we went with exactly the same result, 3-0. So now we were in the quarter-final against Manchester City at Maine Road and stayed in a hotel just outside Manchester, did exactly the same, and drew 0-0. The replay was at Goodison with the same result, 0-0. The third game was at Molineux, so we went through the same routine and won 2-0.

For the Molineux tie Everton defended superbly, with Brian joining Brian Labone in a central resistance which broke the spirit of the City attack. Just before half-time, after good work by Alex Young and Colin Harvey, Brian slotted the ball on one of his occasional forays up-field to Fred Pickering in the box. In one movement Pickering swivelled and crashed the ball past Harry Dowd off the inside of the bar. Derek Temple made the game safe as the Blues moved into the semi-finals. The *Liverpool Post* reported, 'If ever a man deserved to haul his team over another hurdle on the way to Wembley it was Brian Harris. What a terrific worker he was. Whether he was rousing the defence to new heights or lashing the attack into action, his driving force was always apparent.'

Everton soared to their first Wembley final for thirty-three years, defeating Manchester United 1-0 in the semi-final at Burnden Park, Bolton. The Blues were clear value for money and superbly fit, magnificently drilled tactically, with the confidence to make and take their opportunity when it appeared. It had been a hard-fought battle and with about eleven minutes left and thoughts on a replay, a long ball out of defence from Brian found Alex Young, who had melted away from his marker. An onward flick to Derek Temple by Young and the winger shocked a complacent defence with his startling speed. Into his stride he left two defenders trailing and hopped inside to spot Colin Harvey even better placed for a shot. Across went the ball to the incoming youngster. In a moment of supreme challenge the twenty-one-year-old kept his head like a veteran. Resisting the temptation to lash the ball first time he coolly calculated the situation and pulled his shot away from the desperately diving Harry Gregg. Both Young, who hit the post, and Mike Trebilcock might have secured further goals as United desperately sought to save the day with all-out attack. The last kick by a United player might easily have restored equilibrium, for Nobby Stiles shot past Gordon West, pulling the ball just wide of the target and Denis Law dashed in, inches away from the touch that would have painted another story.

How heart-warming to hear a Manchester United manager charitable in defeat, as Matt Busby reflected, 'Everton deserved to win on the day. They were the better team; I could not see us pulling the game off.' Harry Catterick said, 'The boys were magnificent to a man. I was delighted with the way they played the game. It went exactly the way we planned it. We realised they were a strong attacking side and it was our plan to get them coming at us and then to strike on the break. Harvey took his goal brilliantly and Trebilcock could not have fared better in his first cup-tie for the club.' As a senior member of the team Brian had some difficulty in finding the words to express his feelings – 'The greatest day of my life,' he uttered. 'I knew the chances of going to Wembley were running out, but now we are there we want that cup.' Everton's defensive tenacity was encapsulated by a whole-hearted performance from the half-back line of Brian and Jimmy Gabriel alongside Brian Labone. Wherever Bobby

Charlton roamed Gabriel followed in a disciplined performance. The two Brians shared the duties of curbing Law and David Herd. Their understanding was one of the most remarkable features of the game. It is doubtful if the two had ever dovetailed their responsibilities more ably. Experienced observers had never seen them either more dominant or ruthlessly efficient. They read the game accurately and restricted United to speculative shots from outside the box. Seldom had Charlton, Law and Herd been more effectively curbed. It may be truer to say they were not caught on an off-day, so much as having had an off-day created for them.

West; Brown, Wilson; Gabriel, Labone, Harris; Scott, Trebilcock, Young, Harvey, Temple.

When we played Manchester United Jimmy wasn't happy with the same drinking routine for a semi-final, but we went through with it and won. After the game we exchanged good wishes with the United players. I vividly remember shaking hands with George Best, who was injured and didn't play, but gave us his best wishes for the final, by which time he said he would be alongside a swimming pool in Spain with a nice young lady. That gave Jimmy and me positive thoughts about the final – superstition again!

6

A Classic Final

The Blues were the first club in sixty-three years to reach the final without conceding a goal, testament to the durability of Brian and his defensive colleagues. They would have drawn confidence for the big day, having annihilated Sheffield Wednesday 5-1 at Goodison during the opening month of the season. It was one of the finest displays of football many supporters could recall, Alex Young pocketing a superb hat-trick. Harry Catterick sprang a major surprise on the eve of the final, when he retained Cornishman Mike Trebilcock in preference to fit-again leading striker Fred Pickering. It proved an inspired decision.

The plot unfolded with ninety minutes rich in surprise and drama. After four minutes Wednesday's David Ford swept Peter Eustace's long throw across the penalty area for Jim McCalliog to convert home a left-foot shot, which deflected off Ray Wilson's leg. It was the first goal Everton had conceded in over eleven hours of cup football. It looked unlikely to be Lancashire's day as Everton were denied a penalty by Jack Taylor in the first half when Ron Springett's dive upturned Alex Young, as he dribbled the ball past the 'keeper. This feeling was heavily underlined with half an hour to go when Johnny Fantham robbed Young in midfield to burst through a gap past three men. Everton disputed that Brian was obstructed by Ford as Fantham took the ball inside the penalty area and drove powerfully. Gordon West had it covered but could not keep a grip and, as it rebounded from his chest, Ford rushed in and pushed the ball just inside the post for the second. Sheffield Wednesday had played the more incisive football and it seemed that they would upset all the odds as the favourites appeared down and out.

Then out of chaos Everton rose from the dead. Within ninety seconds of that second Wednesday strike, there was Derek Temple soaring like a bird on the left to head a flighted ball from Brian square across the Sheffield goalmouth. Mike Trebilcock struck it first time and the ball flew into the bottom corner of the net wide of Springett's left hand. The game was wide open and swiftly the

Brian is introduced by Brian Labone to Princess Margaret before the Cup final.

balance swung from the white to the red rose. Almost in a twinkling the Toffeemen were level when Brian Labone clashed with Sam Ellis in a crowded area as the two rose from Alex Scott's free-kick. Again it was Trebilcock who met the loose ball first time on the half-volley some fifteen yards out with a right-foot swerving low drive into the bottom corner. In fifteen minutes of inspiration the picture had sensationally altered from 0-2 to 2-2. Swiftly riding this momentum Everton went in search of a winner. Perhaps Wednesday subconsciously relaxed and were caught napping when Gerry Young missed his attempted trap to Colin Harvey's long pass. That let Temple stream home unguarded to pick his spot for the winner with merciless, unforgiving precision. Wednesday responded bravely again over the final quarter of an hour and twice went within inches of forcing extra-time, as Fantham and the overlapping Wilf Smith were near the mark. But Wednesday had had their chance and the final spurt carried more despair than conviction. In that priceless spell the game shifted on its axis. There were five goals in all, the last four in the space of nineteen minutes of a melodramatic plot.

When it was all over there remained one bowed figure, that of Gerry Young, Wednesday's left-half, who had played his heart out and was devastated to be on the losing side – 'The day just flashed by, you don't really remember the occasion, although you should do, you are so pleased to be there. The main thing I remember was that it was a really hot day and we never liked to play in the heat. We scored first and were happy with the way we were playing. We went in 1-0 at half-time and even in the second half we were playing quite nicely, pretty steady when Johnny Fantham made a good run and had a shot. David Ford got the rebound and slotted it in for the second goal. What lost it for us was that, within a few minutes of us scoring Trebilcock knocked the ball into the net to make it 2-1. We needed to defend a 2-0 lead for at least twenty minutes and that for me meant that we lost the impetus all of a sudden. We had two or three young lads in the team – Wilf Smith, Graham Pugh and Sam Ellis – and I think with that inexperience we lost it a bit when we stopped playing easy football. They scored again with Trebilcock, and you think with the score at 2-2 there is going to be extra-time. I remember we had been on the attack and Colin Harvey played a long ball out of the defence, a hopeful ball, which was coming straight for me. I'm a left-footed player and for some reason or other I went on to my right-hand side to trap the ball, but it squeezed underneath. Derek Temple, who was playing on the left-wing, shouldn't have been there, and when I lost the ball he came steaming in and was clean through. When I turned round I knew I didn't have a chance of catching him. I was right behind Derek and remember saying to myself, 'Ron, you've got to save it.' He hit that ball and it went smack into the stanchion, it was a brilliant shot, Ron had no chance. Then it was a matter of pushing bodies forward but we had no chance. It was a shame and very frustrating, but these things happen and you can't dictate when they're going to happen. Everybody in Sheffield knows that I did it, but the folk have been fine, except for one or two. I still get it to this day when I walk through the city. I was walking past Hillsborough recently and this old boy sitting there said to me, 'Do you still have nightmares, Gerry?' But I don't mind that and say, 'Yes, I do!' It was a good final, but obviously would have been better if we had won it, as we hadn't won a final since 1935.'

Everton had snatched the cup for the third time in their history. Only once before at Wembley had a side recovered from an overdraft of two goals, the Matthews final of 1953 when Blackpool emerged from the shadows to win 4-3. In many ways it was like the Matthews final all over again, but on this occasion neither side was inspired by a single individual, it was a magnificent team performance, which Brian Labone endorsed after the final – 'Team spirit did it, this is the team a lot of people have been saying were all individuals who had no spirit to fight. Perhaps this will convince everybody that we have team spirit.

Joy in the Everton faces, dejection in the Wednesday camp. From left to right: Peter Eustace, Johnny Fantham and Sam Ellis, Brian, Tommy Wright and Colin Harvey.

I know it looked a bit bad out there when we were two down and I won't pretend that I wasn't a bit worried, but I thought that if we could get a quick goal we must have a chance. Well Mike got the goal and from that moment we were inspired.'

Within the pattern of a fine sporting match there were several individual cameos. Alex Young, as ever polished, stylish and creative, oozed class as he smoothly stroked the ball about. Derek Temple, quick on acceleration, drifted away from his left flank to wreak havoc down the middle in his role as executioner. He always suggested a goal in his feet, which he duly confirmed when he swept in the winner. Mike Trebilcock confirmed his spurs in the best possible way, with his power and the two goals that swung everything. Behind were Brian and Jimmy Gabriel in the thick of things, more so after the break when Everton, out of necessity pushed forward.

I was just about to celebrate my thirty-first birthday before the cup final and said to myself, 'This could be your last chance.' The great Tom Finney, who is a really nice fellow, gave me the Man of the Match award in his newspaper column, which I am very proud of, as I respect his opinion.

On that dramatic afternoon, Brian's passion for the game shone through with a wonderful display of strong tackling, clever ball control and effective distribution, endorsed in Tom Finney's report: 'Perhaps the most unsung player in the Everton side was Brian Harris, going just as strong at the end as at the start. And using the ball intelligently in defence and attack.'

As the *Liverpool Post* reflected, 'I saw Harris in the dressing room sitting contentedly with a bottle of milk in his hand. For him the occasion must have been almost too much. He knows that he has not much further to go in a top-class football career which has spanned more than ten years, and a winners' medal will be something to treasure. I'm glad he's got it because the service he had rendered to Everton has been magnificent.'

Naturally Brian wasn't going to prepare for the final without completing his superstitious ritual. The party had moved south on the Thursday and Brian was distraught, as Harry Catterick had forbidden his beloved golf in case it interfered with their carefully tabulated preparations. The players did however manufacture a putting competition, but it turned into a farce since no-one could compete with Brian. It proved a welcome distraction, as Ray Wilson was staggered to see the stress etched even in the face of the team's practical joker in the build-up. To consume a bottle of wine on the eve of each tie had proved an innovative way of introducing the two protagonists to the final, although hardly the strategic model.

I know Jimmy Gabriel very well and the way he thinks, I knew he wouldn't be happy with a drink the night before playing at Wembley, so I bought a bottle of Beaujolais and a bottle of Sauterne myself and put them in my case. On the night before a big game you look at your watch, you want to go to sleep but you can't, as it's preying on your mind, so I decided to get my bottle out. Jimmy said, 'I wish I'd got a bottle now,' so I got the other one out, and we both slept brilliantly! Young Tommy Wright, who played right-back, openly said he hardly slept a wink all night. The final was a brilliant day for us all. Playing at Wembley on such an occasion is every player's dream. And to have it come true was the highlight of my career. So many players never get the chance to play in a cup final and for me it was a real pinnacle. We were the clear favourites to win the cup, but struggled to get our rhythm going. I still maintain that I went to clear the ball and Johnny Fantham pulled my shirt back just before he scored the second goal – I don't know how the referee didn't see it. Things didn't look good for us and you can only begin to imagine the language Jimmy on the right-hand side of midfield used on me! We didn't do ourselves or our fans justice on the day, and it was only when we went two goals down that we started to perform. After their second goal we got one back right away thanks to Mike Trebilcock, so we were back in the hunt. Had we not scored so soon we probably would have lost, but we bounced back and played well to win. Harry Catterick found out about our drinking routine afterwards and we had a good laugh with him.

West; Wright, Wilson; Gabriel, Labone, Harris; Scott, Trebilcock, Young, Harvey, Temple.

Stocky Evertonian Eddie Kavanagh invaded the pitch when the Blues equalised and lost his coat in the chase to catch him, exposing a heavyweight pair of braces. A policeman lost his helmet amidst a scene reminiscent of the Keystone cops as Kavanagh was eventually brought down in a mêlée of diving rugby tackles.

I was surprised how the Cup final incident would go down in Wembley history when I put the bobby's hat on. Eddie Kavanagh was a character – he was on Everton's books as an apprentice, played in the junior side, but didn't make the grade – he eventually had seventeen kids. He brought a coach party of forty-two down to the final and got them all in with five tickets! He got slung out of Wembley on the day, got back in somehow, then got thrown out again. I saw him after the game when we got on the coach, I knew he would be waiting for us and there he was, right in front of the coach. I was sitting behind the driver and had a bottle of wine in my hand, which I gave to him. We saw each other a few times after that. When I finished playing I did a bit

As Brian Labone remonstrates with Eddie Kavanagh, Brian tries on the bobby's helmet for size!

of scouting for Bobby Robson at Ipswich, who asked me to watch a young eighteen-year-old lad play for Newcastle at Everton. I went with Beryl and we saw Eddie before the game. Every other word was a swear word and he was on the verge of being abusive, which was quite sad and I had to tell Eddie to behave himself. The young lad? Paul Gascoigne.

In the warm afterglow of the final, the team and management celebrated victory on the Saturday evening with a banquet at Grosvenor House in Park Lane. The players received gold watches from John Moores and all but Warney Cresswell of the 1933 cup-winning side were also in attendance.

Everton Football Club Company Limited
Chairman: Mr. E. Holland Hughes

Finalists:
Football Association Challenge Cup
1965-1966

Celebration Dinner
held at
Grosvenor House, Park Lane, London, W.1

Saturday the Fourteenth of May 1966

Left: The menu card for the Celebration Dinner on Cup final evening at Grosvenor House.

Opposite: Grosvenor House Dinner, Park Lane. Brian and Beryl (on left) are joined by Tommy Wright, Gordon West, Johnny Morrissey, Colin Harvey and their other halves.

Because of my superstition I was the last player to be introduced to Princess Margaret before the game, and she was very nice when I went across to her at the dinner in the evening. She was standing surrounded by her entourage as I approached her and said, 'Hallo madam, how are you, how's things?' She replied in a very posh voice that she was well. When I said jokingly, 'I'd love to give you a kiss,' one of her 'heavies' moved in quick!

Celebrations continued the following day when an estimated quarter of a million fans saluted the cavalcade along the ten-mile route from Allerton Station to St George's Hall, where the players enjoyed a civic reception.

We paraded the cup through Liverpool and were on the top of the bus as we went past Ken Dodd's home at Knotty Ash. He was on the driveway and shouted out at us, 'Copycats, load of bloody copycats!' as Liverpool had won the cup the season before.

On the Monday night Brian was back at St George's Hall for a joint civic dinner to celebrate the performances of Everton and Liverpool, as League champions. Brian and Beryl were returning to their mini after the dinner when they

The Mayor's (Alderman David Cowley) speech. From left to right: Brian Labone, Fred Pickering, Harry Catterick, Brian, Tommy Wright, Gordon West, Alex Scott, Alex Young (partly hidden), Jimmy Gabriel and Colin Harvey.

suffered a terrifying ordeal at the hands of Liverpool 'supporters'. Brian was recognised by a group of over thirty fans as they were getting into the car. They started swearing and kicking and vandalised the mini, trying to turn it over, and rocking it from side to side.

I've never had any trouble from Liverpool fans before, but this was a terrible experience. It took a couple of older Liverpool supporters to fend off the thugs, who were trying to wreck the car. Talk about after the Lord Mayor's Show!

Everton had our League Championship and FA Cup winners' medals mounted on a plaque which had the names of all the players inscribed on it. We had our house broken into on a couple of occasions, but amazingly the medals were overlooked and the police said the burglars must have been Liverpool supporters. I was still very worried and decided to buy two gold chains, Beryl wearing the Championship medal around her neck while I wore the Cup one which I treasured. Because they were quite heavy the links became worn, and in 1987 my son Ian and I went to the local jewellers to repair the links to the FA Cup medal chain. On the way we left the car unattended for a minute and the medal was stolen. It was by the gearbox, someone must have seen it and tried the door. I never believed for a minute the Football Association would agree to strike another Cup medal, but I wrote off and heard nothing for two or three months. Then out of the blue I received a letter to say when the 1987 batch of medals were minted, they would commission an extra one for me. Back home it was reported in the papers and the thief must have had a guilty conscience, as about six months after I received the replica medal the original was hand-delivered through the letter box. I've sold one cup medal and the other I still keep round my neck. It is my most prized footballing possession and I wear it morning, noon and night, it's like wearing thirty-five years of memories. I sold my Championship medal as well to provide something for the grandchildren's future. I didn't realise how much interest there would be for the medals, in memorabilia terms.

Brian Labone cuts the celebration cake outside St George's Hall with Brian looking on, after the Cup final parade.

Brian reflected on his time with the Blues:

I played in every position for Everton, except goalkeeper. When I was initially a winger I ran at the defence and got past them. I did exactly the same thing as a wing-half, so played the same way, relying on my pace and distribution. I was quite happy to play in every position, even at centre-forward and enjoyed them all. I was an attacking, creative wing-half, what you would call a midfield player nowadays who tracked back, I had decent stamina. If I played in defence I'd make a run from the back, but had no problem getting back again. I was two-footed, but my right foot was my stronger, although I played on the left. I could take defenders on either side and cut inside if I wanted to, but it was particularly my pace I relied on.

I guess my humour was good for team morale. We used to go down town and do silly things like look up and say out loud enough for other people to hear, 'He won't jump, will he?' Before we knew it a crowd gathered around us. 'Don't jump,' we'd shout, then we would walk away leaving them gazing up towards the sky!

There is a lot of talk nowadays about a gambling culture amongst players as if it is something new. I was in a card school on the bus for away games when we played for fun, maybe for a pint, but there was a card school of four where they played poker for money, which was more serious. It's because footballers have got time on their hands and get into the habit of going to racecourses etc. It helps relieve the boredom and can bring players closer together as long as it's just a bit of fun.

We trained at Bellefield – training was a lot of passing, fitness and control, I enjoyed it. Harry tended to rely on the experience of the players and of course it's possible to introduce more sophisticated tactics nowadays, as the ball is a lot lighter now. I know training techniques are a lot different today, but I would like to see current players train with the facilities we had, like the ball – if the 'keeper kicked it to the halfway line it was an achievement. Defenders defended on the halfway line, they can't nowadays as it is so much easier to hit the ball over the top of their head. When Joe Royle was a sixteen-year-old I took him under my wing at training as one of the senior pros. I like to think I played a part in helping him develop into becoming a top-class striker.

Bill Shankly had a house overlooking the training ground. We were in a training session once when a ball went over his garden and we never saw it again. He stood at his back step and shouted, 'Unlucky boys, I've got your ball!' Superstition came into the game with a lot of things. I remember once getting a present from a woman, it was a coin. She said, 'You will win this game and you will play well if you throw this up three times and it comes

EVERTON (F.A. Cup-holders): Back row—Barnett, West, Rankin. Middle row—Harris, Pickering, Brown, Labone, Gabriel, Wright, Hurst, Eggleston (trainer). Front row—Morrissey, Scott, Trebilcock, Young, Manager Harry Catterick, Harvey, Temple, Wilson, Ball.

Everton FC proudly show off the FA Cup in the team line-up at the start of the 1966/67 season. From left to right, back row: Barnett, West, Rankin. Middle Row: Harris, Pickering, Brown, Labone, Gabriel, Wright, Hurst, Eggleston (trainer). Front row: Morrissey, Scott, Trebilcock, Young, Catterick (manager), Harvey, Temple, Wilson, Ball.

down heads.' I didn't tell anyone and sat on the toilet in the dressing room before the game for ages until I got three heads! The year before the Cup final I wore my shirt outside my shorts for the first time. Everton won the game and I played well, so I carried on wearing my shirt like that – it was all down to superstition again.

7

A Fresh Challenge
1966-1967

Despite the glorious end to the season, Brian was in and out of the side at the beginning of the 1966/67 campaign. With Colin Harvey occupying his favourite half-back slot, Brian sought an interview with Harry Catterick to discuss his prospects. He played against West Brom but was dropped for the following game against Leeds to allow Jimmy Gabriel to return from injury. He was then ominously left out of the party which travelled to Denmark for the Cup-Winners' Cup tie against Aalborg at the end of September. He was reinstated when the Blues were under strength for the Newcastle home fixture at the beginning of October. It was his 358th and last game for Everton and typically Brian, the inveterate competitor, gave it his all albeit in an unfamiliar role. In the absence of the injured Fred Pickering, Brian was drafted into the attack, wearing the number 10 shirt. Albert Bennett put the visitors into the lead in the first half, but it was nearly all Everton in the second. Against the experienced trio of Keith Kettleborough, Jim Iley and Bobby Moncur, Brian toiled hard to make an impression and nearly scored with a spectacular diving header which was ruled off-side. Jimmy Gabriel finally equalised in the seventieth minute and, according to one report, 'Harris is entitled to think he did well enough in a position which at the moment is a problem.'

West; Wright, Wilson; Gabriel, Labone, Harvey; Temple, Ball, Young, Harris, Morrissey.

I picked up a hamstring injury on a pre-season tour of Ireland at the beginning of the 1966/67 season, which sidelined me for two months. By the time I was fit again things had changed. John Hurst had broken through from the Youth side, Alan Ball had arrived from Blackpool and made a huge impact, and Harry was drastically rebuilding the side. I'd have been quite happy to finish my playing career with Everton, when out of the blue Harry called me into his office and asked if I would be interested in signing for

Cardiff City. It was only because I had to make a quick decision that I came to South Wales, a move which, looking back, Beryl and I never regretted.

Catterick spoke trenchantly in support of Brian – 'Harris was not on offer, but recently expressed a wish to me that he would like a regular place in the League side, which was something I could not guarantee. It was only because of his loyal service to Everton over the years that the directors, with reluctance, agreed to let him go. I would much rather have kept him, but realise a move would be to Harris' benefit and because of his wonderful service I offered no objection.' The fee involved was £10,000 and Brian signed transfer forms on 14 October 1966. He had received two benefit cheques during his time at Everton, one for £750 and the other for £1,000.

I went down to see Jimmy Scoular more out of courtesy than anything else. I didn't know much about the area even though I'd played at Cardiff once or twice. Like people think Merseyside is mainly docks and pubs, I thought South Wales consisted of coal-mines and docks. Jimmy said they were playing Plymouth the next game and, if I wanted to sign, I'd be going with them. Beryl told me that if I wanted to make the move, then she'd be quite happy about it if it helped my career. If I'd had the weekend to think about it I wouldn't have signed, particularly in view of Cardiff's low League position at the time, but I suppose I wanted to show everyone that I was still capable of holding down a first-team place and doing a good job because, since the age of thirty, I'd been written off every time I'd had an injury. It was hard to leave because I had so many memories, but it was better for me to get a regular slot in a lower division side than just languish in Everton's reserves, so I signed. I played four games at the start of that season, so the FA Cup final was not quite my last game for Everton although, two days short of my thirty-first birthday, it was a fitting finale.

I regretted the move for a brief instant at half-time in that first match at Plymouth. We were 4-0 down and eventually lost 7-1. After the game Jimmy said, 'Anything I can do for you?' I replied, 'Yes, you can rip up my contract.' When I got back to Everton on the Monday, Gordon West and the rest of the lads were wearing black ties! I remember saying to Beryl when I got home that the glamour times were over, with no more foreign trips such as the Everton tour to Canada and USA early in my career. But then came our Cup Winners' Cup which took us all over Europe and was just like a dream, it was incredible. We also went on a close of season tour of Australia and New Zealand. There were other European trips in my four and a half years at Ninian Park so, through my involvement in football, I've been lucky enough to have travelled all over the world except to South America. I was the senior player and everyone else looked up to me, which was a bit strange at first, but I really enjoyed my time there. It was a very different set-up from Everton. The club was obviously not as big, but that made the success we had even more satisfying, because it was so unexpected.

At the end of my first season (1966/67) at Cardiff John Charles came round to our house and asked me if I wanted to go on tour with him. I said, 'Hold on a minute, I'll just get my case.' I wasn't really keen! His International XI went on a six-week tour of Zambia and Mauritius, when John was player-manager at Hereford. We had some good players on tour, including the Allchurch brothers and Terry Medwin. I was John's room-mate and he was a smashing guy. Every day we would train for about half an hour, have a run on the beach and get back to the hotel in time for the bar to open! We would have a drink and John would usually ask me for a large whisky and coke. At the end of the evening John had a habit of getting into bed, switching the TV on and falling asleep. He would put his money on top of the bedside cabinet that separated our beds. While he was asleep I would reimburse myself for all the drinks I bought him. This went on for about a week, and at the end of the week John said to me, 'Brian, I've been room-mates with some of the greatest players in the world from Italy, etc. You've been the best mate I've ever had.' I asked, 'What do you mean?' He said, 'Well, If I want a large whisky and coke, it's there and I never have to pay for it.' I never told him the truth until I played golf at Buxton years later and John was there. We all had a drink after the game and John started talking about the tour and what a brilliant room-mate I was. When I told him the truth he said, jokingly, 'You bastard!' I replied, 'It's taken me all these years for the right moment to tell you.'

One night on the tour we were invited by the Royal Navy to a dinner at a spacious club not far from our hotel. John, who liked to sing a little bit, went on stage. He sang for about ten minutes and came off to loud applause from everyone in the club. About ten minutes later we were all sitting round our table when this guy wearing his Navy gear came to our table and asked who had just sang on stage. He pointed a finger at each one of us, but no-one admitted to it until he spoke to John, the last person. When John nodded he poured a pint of beer all over John, turned away and made his way back to his table where his wife and friends were sitting. We noticed they were all laughing so John, after seeing this, shouted to his brother Melvyn and we all walked over to this guy's table – there was John, brother Melvyn behind and the rest of us tagging on. As he arrived at the table John picked up a pint of beer and threw it over the navy guy and his wife. As he did this a lady came across to John and asked him for a dance to defuse the situation. They went on to the dance floor, we went back to our table, not realising that Mel was keeping his eye on this guy. The next thing we knew Melvyn had jumped up and shouted to John that he was walking towards the dance floor. John separated himself from the lady just as this bloke arrived. John wasn't the sort of person to cause trouble, but as this bloke tried to take a swing at him, John side-stepped him and whacked him one – he took off horizontally and ended flat on his back! John made his way to the stage, stopped the music, apologised to everybody, said goodbye, and we all left – that was the end of the entertainment for the evening.

Whilst unable to regain a place in the top division of League football, City found an alternative outlet for their talents at the highest level in the European Cup-Winners' Cup.

As time went on Cardiff got stronger and stronger, with quality players like John Toshack and Brian Clark and, in those days, with no disrespect to Chester, Hereford, Wrexham and Barry, we only had to beat them to get into Europe.

March 1968 v. Middlesbrough. Captain Courageous injures his ankle trying to prevent a goal in the 3-2 Cardiff victory at Ayresome Park.

8

Captain Brian Chases the European Dream
1968-1969

The Bluebirds gained more or less perpetual entry to the Cup-Winners' Cup through the Welsh Cup and shocked the football world in the 1967/68 season by reaching the semi-finals. Brian had played in his first Welsh Cup final in May 1967, when City defeated Wrexham 2-1. A goal from Norman Dean and an own goal by George Showell secured their place in Europe. In September 1967 at Dublin, in the opening round of the Cup-Winners' Cup, Shamrock Rovers threatened at one stage to make the Bluebirds' cup crusade a brief one. The home side pushed forward from the onset and Bobby Gilbert deservedly scored the first goal after seventeen minutes. Cardiff fought their way back into the game and from a Barrie Jones corner link-man Peter King equalised. The return leg at Ninian Park was not a classic, but John Toshack and Bobby Brown, with a penalty made sure of further progress. Holland was the next port of call, this time against NAC Breda, very much an unknown quantity. Once again the opposition went into an early lead, but a clever one-two with Bobby Brown created an opening for Peter King to convert despite a nagging injury, as the youthful Dutch side were held to a 1-1 draw. Brown drifted free of his marker to sweep Cardiff into the lead after three minutes of the second leg and, when Barrie Jones danced through to add a second, it looked as if Cardiff were home and dry. However, Bob Wilson allowed a tame long-range effort to slip between his hands to bring the Dutchmen back into the game. City regained their composure and late goals from Malcolm Clarke and Toshack sealed Breda's fate.

Jimmy Scoular had by now devised an effective way of playing the away leg, with an extra defensive player, usually Malcolm Clarke, and his plan worked to perfection on a number of occasions. A significant Scoular signing in February 1968 was Brian Clark from Huddersfield, a proven goalscorer, although he was ineligible for the European games. The Bluebirds had reached the quarter-finals

March 1968 v. Moscow Torpedo. Brian joins the attack to head narrowly wide during the tie at Ninian Park.

for the second time in their history and were determined to go one stage further when drawn against Moscow Torpedo. There was nostalgic talk amongst the older Cardiff supporters of the great Torpedo side that weaved its patterns all over the UK in 1945 and put ten goals past the Bluebirds. In March 1968 a surprisingly modest Ninian Park gate of 30,000 for the first leg witnessed a header from Barrie Jones shortly before half-time to give City a slim advantage.

The Russian capital was experiencing sub-zero temperatures and the pitch at the Lenin Stadium was nine feet deep in snow in places when the team arrived for the return leg, so the tie was switched to Torpedo's summer ground in the cotton-growing area of Tashkent, the capital of Uzbekistani, 2,000 miles away from their Moscow home. It was a city in the heart of Asia on a triangle of the world that was only 300 miles from the borders of China, Afghanistan and Northern India. The squad left Cardiff on the morning of Thursday 14 March and, after a two-day stopover in Moscow, arrived in time to prepare for the match on Tuesday 19 March. Moscow Dynamo were conducting a training session at the ground when the players went to have a look. The legendary Russian Lev Yashin was doing his stuff in goal on a pitch that looked superb in the sun, quite a contrast from what they left behind in Moscow. When the

Bluebirds arrived for the game the stadium was packed with a capacity crowd of 68,000, generating the atmosphere of a cup final. City's star was Bob Wilson, with a brilliant display of goalkeeping. He was only beaten by a single goal to leave the tie requiring a play-off. Leaving hours after the game and catching a connecting flight in Moscow to London, by the time their coach had made its way back to Cardiff the party had been away from home for almost a week and covered a little less than 7,000 miles. It was the longest journey ever made by a European club.

UEFA decided the third match would take place in Augsberg, forty miles from Munich in Bavaria. City were in trouble as centre-half lynch-pin Don Murray was injured and, although he had treatment throughout the journey to Germany, he was unfit to play. Reserve defender Richie Morgan, who had not even appeared in a League match, was drafted into the team along with four other reserves. After soaking up pressure in the first half an hour, two minutes from half-time, John Toshack who won everything in the air, headed down Graham Coldrick's long pass to Norman Dean – another reserve – sprinting into the penalty area. Dean's thunderous shot dealt a fatal blow to the Russians' hopes

Everton v. Moscow Torpedo, March 1968. Brian shakes hands with Torpedo captain Schustikov in Tashkent.

March 1968 – Cardiff's wandering minstrels return from Tashkent. From left to right: Steve Derrett, Gary Bell, Peter King, Brian and Leighton Phillips.

at a psychologically crucial time for the Bluebirds. In a nerve-racking second half, Torpedo attacked incessantly. This was an occasion for men of heart and Cardiff possessed them, none more so than the stout blue wall of defenders, which sent City through to the semi-final on a 2-1 aggregate. At the core was Brian, asserting himself, driving his men on and nurturing young Morgan, who more than held his own against international Streltsov. To add a further frisson of tension to the proceedings, an injury time save by heroic Bob Wilson from Gerskovich, the little inside-forward who had scored in Tashkent, was inspirational.

Wilson; Coldrick, Ferguson; Clarke, Morgan, Harris; Jones, Dean, King, Toshack, Bird.

When we played Torpedo at Ninian Park, as captain I went into the referee's room prior to the game with my opposite number. We shook hands and their captain kept making strange hand gestures, which looked to me like he was

April 1968 – City players celebrate on the team bus after a 1-1 draw in Hamburg. Brian and Bobby Ferguson are in front with scorer of the goal Norman Dean and Malcolm Clarke sitting behind. Behind them are Graham Coldrick and Richie Morgan.

being threatening, then he prodded me on the top of the body. The referee was Herr Fritz, a German and I couldn't speak any German and he didn't speak English, so we couldn't work out what he was trying to say. I tried to ignore him, but he was ranting away in Russian so I said, 'Hey mate, where I come from, that's provocative.' But he didn't understand a word I said. We went off to Moscow with a 1-0 lead, but it snowed like hell, so we went to Tashkent, several hours away by plane, and played in front of about 70,000 fans. Before the game started their captain prodded me again, which really got on my nerves. I thought he wanted to pick a fight with me and, even when I was getting close to him on the field, he was giving me stick. They won 1-0 and for the replay in Germany we took a lad from Cardiff University to act as interpreter, won 1-0 and our supporters went berserk. I looked towards their dressing room and saw the captain still shouting at me. I told the interpreter to go and sort him out and he returned to tell me he was trying to ask me out for a drink after the game. He'd been trying to ask me for a drink for three games but in a different sign language to how we would do it! He was in the

Russian Army and, when we got back to the hotel, he joined us and we had a good laugh together. In fact the lads went out and left the two of us in the bar at the hotel until about two o'clock in the morning. I could have escalated the cold war there and then, but we had a good time, even though we couldn't understand what either of us was saying!

Cardiff were pitted against SV Hamburg for the semi-final, quality opposition with a number of German internationals in their squad, including Uwe Seeler and Willi Schulz, although both were injured for the first leg in the Volkspark Stadium. Schulz's absence in the Hamburg defence proved a telling factor which the Bluebirds, with startling poise and concentration, were quick to exploit. After just four minutes Peter King pushed a short pass to Norman Dean, whose burst of acceleration created a yawning gap in the opposition defence. As defenders converged on him Dean picked his spot low and wide of Ozcan, the 'keeper. It was a fantasy goal of precision from a player who was clearly reserving his best performances for the European stage. The Germans, stunned into action, started to stretch the City defence with clever passing and movement at pace. For the remainder of the first half efforts rained down on the Welsh defence and Hamburg were not to be denied. A shot by Sandmann from point-blank range equalised the score midway through the second half

Everton v. Hamburg, May 1968. Brian greets Uwe Seeler before the Ninian Park tie.

after sustained pressure. Once again a rousing defensive performance enabled the Bluebirds to hold out for a magnificent draw. Brian, a 24-carat big game player, a connoisseur of the moment, was outstanding and Bob Wilson again made a series of magnificent saves.

The second leg at Ninian Park on 1 May 1968 saw Brian exchange pennants with the returning Uwe Seeler in front of 43,070 passionate fans. The Bluebirds tore into the Hamburg defence from the off and the German defence, again missing Schulz, was made to look highly suspect. Pressure was exerted by the lively Barrie Jones, Dean and Toshack, and the side were driven on in midfield by the tireless Peter King and Malcolm Clarke. Norman Dean maintained his wonderful European record with a goal after ten minutes following an incisive run from Clarke. Although Hamburg equalised within five minutes when Hoenig flashed home a drive into the roof of the net, Cardiff exerted pressure up to the interval. The second half continued in the same vein and a goal from Uwe Seeler with half an hour to go came against the run of play. It was something of a fluke as Seeler, a yard inside the penalty area and with his back to goal, chipped the ball up and lobbed it blindly with his left foot, only to see the ball swing in under the far post. In truth it could have gone anywhere, as one commentator confirmed, 'It might have landed in Jutland or Timbuktu for all the German captain might have known.' However, that goal stirred the Germans into greater self-belief and belatedly they showed more cohesion as they pushed forward. The game opened up as both sides tired and Ninian Park was invaded by jubilant supporters when Brian equalised with a header from Jones' cross ten minutes from the end. With the prospect of a play-off the crowd was ecstatic, only to be brought down to earth in the cruellest possible way with the very last kick of the game in injury time.

Hoenig controlled a long pass out of defence and broke quickly some forty yards between three Cardiff defenders. A curling right-foot shot with a nasty spin on it from about eighteen yards tricked Bob Wilson, who dived to the far post with the ball apparently covered. The shot spun through Wilson's fingers and trickled gently over the line, as he made a despairing backward lunge to save it. Of course it was Wilson, as much as anybody, who had helped take Cardiff so far along the European dream. Uwe Seeler had just one chance and took it – for the rest, big Don Murray played him out of sight, but City's romantic journey was over.

Wilson; Carver, Ferguson; Clarke, Murray, Harris; Jones, Dean, King, Toshack, Lea.

City had won a new pride, even if success was denied them. Where Brian had strived tirelessly to propel his former club into the latter stages of European

1968 – Cardiff's defensive duo Don Murray and Brian talk tactics with manager Jimmy Scoular.

competition, it is ironic that his most successful campaigns took place away from Everton.

The highlight for me at Cardiff was playing in Hamburg. It was a great game to play in and incredible for a Second Division team to draw a side of their stature away. In the second leg 'Harold' Bob Wilson dropped a clanger and that was the end of it. We should have beaten them at home and knew it was our best chance to get to the final. To lose to a last-minute goal was a sickener, the worst possible feeling. It was a tremendous thrill for me to play top-class opposition again, as I didn't expect it. Everton never reached those heights in Europe, which is strange. They were great occasions when you look back, although you're not really aware of the significance at the time. Reaching the semi-finals of a major European competition with any side would have been special, but with a team like Cardiff it was really something. Who knows what might have been had we actually made it to the final, but to be that close meant an awful lot to the supporters in Wales.

9

Other Cardiff Memories
1968-1971

FC Porto provided stern opposition for the Bluebirds' next Cup-Winners' Cup sortie during the 1968/69 season. Cardiff deservedly took the lead in the first leg at Ninian Park in the twenty-fourth minute with a glorious header from John Toshack. Barrie Jones gained possession on the wing and sent over an inch-perfect cross for Tosh to soar high and head into the far corner of the net from about ten yards. Ronnie Bird scored the second with a penalty in the fifty-first minute after Toshack had been brought down by Acacio. City looked to be coasting to victory when international Pinto pulled a goal back in the sixtieth minute. Pinto then headed a dramatic equaliser in controversial circumstances.

Their second goal was diabolical. When the winger crossed the ball was clearly over the byline. Perhaps we shouldn't have stopped and played to the whistle, but the ball was so obviously out of play it was only a question of awarding a goal-kick. We were horrified when we realised the linesman hadn't flagged and we never recovered from that.

Cardiff were unfortunate to lose a very physical second leg in October 1968. A goal from John Toshack reduced the margin after Porto scored twice. Having given a penalty earlier in the game only to reverse his decision, the referee finally awarded the Bluebirds a spot-kick in the last minute, much to the home crowd's disgust. It was too little too late. As Toshack took the kick the fans did everything to distract him and he missed. At the end of the match the crowd invaded the pitch and the police went into action with a baton charge. Amidst chaotic scenes Bob Wilson, who was sitting on the bench for this tie, took a crack on the head for his troubles. City had been evicted at the first hurdle 4-3 on aggregate.

The remainder of the 1968/69 season proved a depressing one for Brian, as injury restricted his first-team appearances to 17 in the League. When he returned to match fitness he found Steve Derrett barring his way and conceded

Fred Davies, Les Lea and Brian arrive at Adelaide Airport for the start of City's summer tour of Australia, 1968.

the captaincy to Don Murray. However, Brian proved his boots had yet to grow mould with a glorious return to the side at the start of the 1969/70 season. He held his place throughout, missing only three of forty-two League games, and those because of injury. He was back to his best, an authoritative influence on a defence which turned out one of the meanest goals-against-records in the Second Division.

Following another Welsh Cup triumph the Bluebirds hit their record score in Europe in the first round of the Cup-Winners' Cup. In September 1969 they slammed the Norwegian part-timers of Mjondalen 7-1 in the away leg, with two goals each from Toshack and Brian Clark. Reserve striker Sandy Allan bagged a hat-trick in the 5-1 second-leg win, Peter King notching the other two goals. Once again interest was short-lived as a disastrous 3-0 away defeat to Turkish Cup-holders Goztepe Izmir in the second round put paid to the Bluebirds'

1969 – Cardiff summer tour of Africa. From left to right, standing: Phillips, King, Davies, Harris, Sharp, Murray, Morgan, Scoular, Carver. Front: Lea, Clayton (trainer), Bell, Bird, Clark, Allan.

Cardiff v. QPR, September 1969. Dan Murray, who was City's defensive rock alongside Brian, tackles Rodney Marsh during a 4-2 home victory.

European aspirations. A strike from Ronnie Bird in the home leg reduced the deficit to 3-1 on aggregate.

A club record fee of £35,000 was paid to Coventry City for Ian Gibson at the start of the 1970/71 season and, during the early part the Bluebirds again enjoyed success in Europe. In the first round of the Cup-Winners' Cup, they eviscerated Cypriot side Pezoporikos Larnaca 8-0 at home, Tosh and Brian Clark helping themselves to two goals each. FC Nantes were then vanquished 7-2 on aggregate in October 1970, Tosh scoring another three times over the two legs. The transfer of Toshack in November 1970 upset Bluebird fans, although it was inevitable he would migrate to a higher level. City accepted a fee of £110,000 from Liverpool and, in order to placate the fans, paid £40,000 to Sheffield Wednesday for his replacement, Alan Warboys, on Christmas Eve. Warboys, however, had been signed too late to play in the quarter-final, which brought the draw everyone had coveted from the moment Cardiff first became involved in the European scene. The Division Two side would play the mighty Real Madrid in the quarter-finals.

In March 1971 Ninian Park was packed with 47,500 Bluebird supporters, who will never forget the sight of seventeen-year-old Nigel Rees crossing for Clark to nod past Real 'keeper Borja. Brian's place had been taken by Leighton Phillips,

Cardiff City FC 1970-71. From left to right, back row: Derrett, Parsons, Pethard, Lea. Middle row: Sutton, Phillips, Lewis, Eadie, Davies, Morgan, Carver, Sharp. Front row: Woodruff, Toshack, Clark, King, Murray, Harris, Bird, Bell.

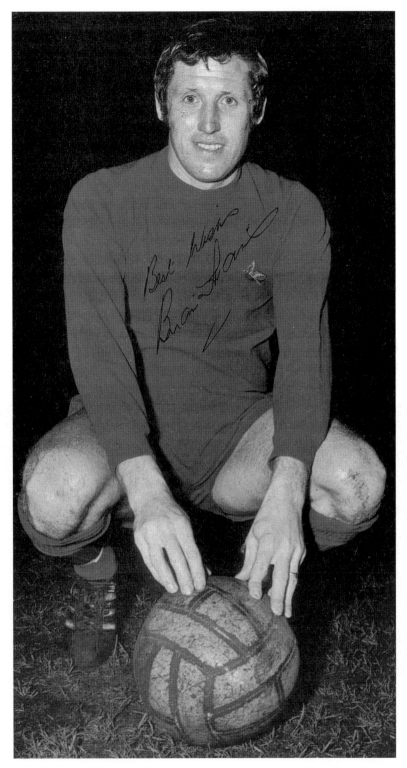

1971 – Brian in Cardiff colours.

but he was delighted to make a substitute appearance in the away leg. The Bluebirds showed great defensive determination in the imposing Bernabeu Stadium, holding the Spaniards to 0-0 in the first half, and seemed in relatively little danger. After the interval however, Real encouraged their supporters with an early revival. They scored twice within a minute, the first a volley by Velasquez and the second a solid drive from Fleitas-Miranda. As City battled to regroup the affair became increasingly ill-tempered and they were unable to prevent the opposition tightening their grip for a 2-0 victory.

Eadie; Carver, Bell; Sutton, Murray, Phillips; King, Gibson, Clark, Woodruff, Rees. Sub. Harris

I came on with about fifteen minutes to go. I had been injured and was desperate to be involved, and Scoular put me on in the hope that my experience would influence the game. I remember after the match one of the directors, when he realised I had played for Everton, took me round the ground and invited me into the trophy room – not a bad collection of trophies!

Brian and Ian Gibson soak up the atmosphere in the Bernabeu Stadium before the cup tie with Real Madrid, 1971.

By the end of Brian's first season at Cardiff relegation had been avoided, albeit the club finished a lowly twentieth in Division Two. It was hardly coincidental that Brian's arrival brought equilibrium, stability and experience to the back line and an improving trend in the League. City ended the 1967/68 campaign in thirteenth place, improving to fifth position in 1968/69 and seventh in 1969/70. The club were unable to repeat their European success in either the FA or League Cup. During Brian's tenure they never progressed beyond the fourth round of either competition. Brian's last season was his most successful in the League at Cardiff, as the Bluebirds just missed out on promotion, finishing in third place. He did struggle with injury problems and made his 202nd and last appearance as substitute in the 1-0 defeat of Bolton in April 1971 at Ninian Park. The Scoular years, with the side marshalled expertly on the pitch by Brian, are etched in City folklore for embracing some of the finest moments in the Bluebirds' chequered history. Brian reflects on his spell at City:

The change in tactics and style of play during the time I was playing the game didn't really affect me, compared to who I was playing with. It was only when I went to Cardiff that I lost a bit of pace and played a more defensive role dovetailing with Don Murray, the centre-half. He went for everything down the middle and if he missed it, I got it – I would just slide round the back of him. The fact that I could read the game well with my experience helped. Apart from the Cup-Winners' Cup, we had some other great games, like playing in front of 37,000 at Ninian Park against Manchester City in the fourth round of the FA Cup when Joe Mercer was manager (February 1967). We drew 1-1 and in the replay at Maine Road lost 3-1, but didn't disgrace ourselves. It was good to have the opportunity to pit your wits against a First Division side again.

Cardiff's jewel in the crown was, of course, John Toshack, who made his senior debut as a sixteen-year-old in the 1965/66 season.

John had a good touch on the ball – he wasn't that athletic, but could control the ball well, trap it, pass it and finish well. Bobby Robson asked me about him when he was managing Fulham. I said he had good control, headed the ball well, was fit and there wasn't much weight on him, but Tosh didn't want to go at the time. Then Mr Liverpool (Bill Shankly) phoned up and asked me about him and I told him the same. When Tosh went up to Liverpool for the first time I said to him, 'Make sure the missus has got a nice blue top on, they're mad on those colours up there.' Up they went on the train and all the supporters, who knew he was coming, were waiting for him at Lime Street station with their red tops on. He phoned me on his return not very happy about my joke. Jimmy Scoular's paint-stripping direct style of management was legendary.

Jimmy was a shouter, he shouted at everyone. But that was his style and you became used to it and got on with it. I played against him at Newcastle and knew he was a hard man in his day. In the five-a-side games I would usually play against him and he would often go over the top. He treated me differently not because I was captain, but where I came from. He had respect for me, at least he listened to what I said, but only after he had his say first! He used to ask me to hang about after training to discuss tactics and team selection. He relied on me and was in the habit of making the ideas that we adopted his, not mine.

I stayed behind doing a bit of running on a dark afternoon once when the groundsman was out working on the pitch. Jimmy went over to give him a hand with the mower and let him have a rest as it was raining a bit. 'Go and get yourself a cup of tea,' he said. When the groundsman went back Jimmy had only moved it about five yards and was sweating very heavily. 'I don't know how you move it, it's so heavy,' he said. 'It's a motorised one, you just press the button here,' replied the groundsman. When he saw Jimmy coming across the park he'd switched it off!

There was a good team spirit we developed at Cardiff, much along the same lines as at Everton. We socialised together and used to say we were going to a golf driving range on a Thursday night. It was actually an excuse for going to a club in Cardiff near the County Cricket Club!

10

Newport Beckons and Football Management
1971-1974

Being asked to save Fourth Division side Newport County from falling out of the Football League in the early seventies was like trying to save a stricken ship in stormy seas. In 1970/71 County reached their lowest ebb since re-election to the Football League in 1932, failing to win any of their first twenty-three matches, collecting just three points, and looked to be on their way out of the League. A fighting comeback in the second half of the season, spearheaded by general manager Billy Lucas, did persuade the Football League at the AGM to give them one more chance. The resurgence in form was not enough to prevent County's third successive re-election application, but that was all they needed. In the summer of 1971 Newport whistled down the road to Cardiff for Brian in an attempt to steady the ship.

I had an injury at Cardiff and Leighton Phillips took my position. At my age I wanted to play regularly and Newport County asked me if I wanted to become player-coach. That first season was probably going to be our last in the League if we had to seek re-election again. It was a challenge to help provide the club with as much success as I had as a player and things went really well. I enjoyed a few games there and extended my career, after all I got to pick the side!

It was an inauspicious start for the club's only close-season signing, as in September 1971 Brian dislocated his shoulder against Northampton Town. Billy Lucas experimented by playing him in midfield as well as at the back in an effort to reverse a disconcerting slide in form and, in order to tap into his knowledge and expertise, Brian was appointed assistant manager in February 1972. A 3-2 victory at Colchester in April 1972 eased any lingering re-election worries and a spurt of eleven points from the last six games took County to fourteenth position. Amidst predominantly local young players, Brian's steadying influence was a major reason for the improvement in form during the campaign. It was a culture shock playing in basement football for the first time and Brian had to adapt quickly. His stated aim was for his side to succeed by playing attractive football, but he soon realised that it was sometimes necessary to compromise those beliefs in the interests of securing a result, reflected in comments he made at the time:

We play more entertaining football away from home because the pressure is off us to a degree – nobody expects us to do well but we don't get the results. However, we seem to achieve more by uncomplicated tactics which pressure forces us to use at home – the long ball into the opposing area, dull but necessary. I have been used to playing constructive football throughout my career and it is frustrating not always being able to do so.

On 26 August 1972 club captain Brian reached a notable landmark with his 500th Football League appearance against Colchester United, joining a select band of eleven, who at the time had made more appearances – John Connelly, Jack and Bobby Charlton, Frank Large, Jim Iley, Terry Paine, Peter Dobing, Dave Mackay, Alan Mullery, Colin Taylor and former colleague Jimmy Gabriel. His teammates thought he had reached the landmark the previous Saturday and presented him with a wristwatch before the kick-off. Brian promised not to wear it until after the Colchester game!

The 1972/73 season, Newport's Diamond Jubilee Year, was the most successful since the war and neutrals throughout the country were delighted to see County make a powerful bid for promotion. Playing attractive football – one of Brian's most satisfying games in a managerial sense – at League leaders Southport in January 1973, County were worthy victors with goals from Andy White and Robert Summerhayes in what was described as one of their greatest displays in recent years. A number of Brian's contacts from the north were there to see County prove that Fourth Division football was well worth watching. The side won universal praise and it marked a symbolic watershed for the club, which had finally buried old images of failure.

County faded slightly during the Easter period, but a battling 4-3 victory against Bury in the last game saw them in fourth place with fifty-six points, the highest total of their League career. Aldershot were one point behind with one game to play. County fans agonised for almost a week until Aldershot drew their final game at Stockport and pipped Newport to the fourth promotion place by the ricepaper margin of 0.12 of a goal.

Away from the League, in November 1972 Brian scored twice in the first round of the FA Cup against Alton Town, his only goals for County. Alton conceded a penalty late in the game which handed Brian the opportunity for a first senior hat-trick, but he declined in favour of Roddy Jones, the leading goalscorer, who successfully converted to make the scoreline 5-1. Other scorers were Andy White and Willie Brown.

In two years the club's average attendance had doubled and hopes were high for the 1973/74 season. In the event, it was a relatively disappointing campaign, with influential players Len Hill and Steve Aizlewood frequently injured, as well as Brian himself, and new signings Brian Godfrey and Harold Jarman struggling to find a consistent rhythm. Brian was formally appointed player-manager in January 1974 when Billy Lucas was made general manager and County finished the season in ninth place.

Soon after I was appointed manager I spent a couple of days watching Leeds United train. They were top of the League and I had met Don Revie through John Charles, so I thought I had nothing to lose by giving him a ring. He

Newport County FC 1973-74. From left to right, back row: Summerhayes, S. Aizlewood, Payne, Macey, Jones, Thomas, Copeland. Third row: Jarman, Crosse, White, Swain, Guilfoyle, Rogers, Fisher, Godfrey. Second row: Screen, White, Passey, Brown, Harris, Coldrick, Hill, Hooper. Front row: Channing, M. Aizlewood.

suggested I came up to Leeds to watch them train. I sat with Don, watching Les Cocker put the players through their paces – jogging and sprinting, all quite impressive. Then Les gave them a rest while he put eleven oil drums on the pitch in all the positions. 'What's all this, Don?' I asked. He said it was to give the players confidence of going past stationary objects and crossing the ball. So I went back to Newport and put my players through their paces. Three days later Don phoned me and asked how things were going. I said it was going really well and they were getting a lot fitter. He asked me how we had gone on with the oil drums. I said, 'Well we got beat 5-1!' They used to say if there was a night game and a big cheer went up, the night workers nearby would ask, 'Have County scored?' The reply was, 'No, the meat pies have just arrived!' It was a difficult job at Newport with little funds to strengthen the squad.

I remember one Friday in the early days I needed to sort a few things out with Billy Lucas, who was also a publican at the time, about the game the next day. We had been training and I was in the car with John Macey when we came back to Somerton Park through the gates. I saw Billy coming out of the ground and got John to stop the car, so that I could have a quick word with him about the team. I said, 'Bill, I need a couple of minutes with you to sort out the team for tomorrow.' Billy said, 'Sorry matey,' – which is what he called everybody – 'I can't stop now, Edie's just rung me, the Guinness is off, I've got to get back to the Talisman and sort it out.' The only way I could speak to him about the game was to go back to the pub with him. It was a bit different from Everton!

I wasn't really influenced by anyone I played under when I became a manager. I had my own way of running the team and wouldn't shout at the players, but would encourage them. I did it my own way and joined in at five-a-sides, it was a hands-on approach. If any of the players had anything to say, I was happy for them to say it. I think being player-manager helped, because as captain I could boss them around on the park. I tended to play a 4-3-3 system, but occasionally dabbled in 4-4-2.

In April 1974 Brian was granted a long overdue testimonial match at Somerton Park.

I didn't have a testimonial at Everton and, by the time I had moved to Newport, Billy Bingham had become the manager there. I'd always got on well with Billy and he offered to bring the full Everton team down to Newport. Dixie Deans kicked the match off, we all got round the centre-circle, put the ball on the spot and Dixie stubbed his foot! He was a hell of a character and I think he may have had a few bevvies. When he had a benefit dinner once I met him at the bar and he asked me how much I earned playing for Everton.

BRIAN HARRIS

Testimonial Match

(Official Souvenir Programme)

at Somerton Park, Newport.
Wednesday 10th April 1974, Kick-off 7.30 p.m.

NEWPORT COUNTY v EVERTON

50p

*Programme
Fee Includes
Admission*

April 1974 – Brian's testimonial match programme.

When I said £20 per week he said, 'I only got £10 per week, with no goal bonuses.' With all those goals he got just a tenner, irrespective of the number of goals he scored. It was in the days of the maximum wage and I think he was a bit upset I was getting double what he had been paid.

In the first half Everton played Newport County and for the second we introduced some stars. John Charles played and Bobby Charlton took penalties at half-time. There was a crowd of over 6,000, but the two guys who organised it for me did a runner and I ended up with virtually nothing.

Newport held Everton to a creditable 3-3 draw. Brian linked up with Jimmy Gabriel, by then a Brentford player, at the centre of the County defence to

April 1974 – Dixie Dean kicks off the testimonial match, watched by Brian.

restrict Everton to goals from Mick Buckley, Mike Bernard and Bob Latchford. Newport replied through Willie Brown, Harold Jarman and Andy White. An entertaining penalty competition at half-time saw John Charles and Graham Coldrick come out on top. Whilst Bobby Charlton scored all six of his penalty efforts, his partner Barry John could only put the ball past John Macey three times.

Macey; Screen, Passey; Godfrey, Gabriel, Harris; Woodruff, Hill, R. Jones, Brown, White.

Brian finally drew the curtain down on an illustrious career at the end of the 1973/74 season following injury. At nearly thirty-nine he was the oldest player in League football at the time and his testimonial match appearance was the last occasion Brian donned a County shirt. He had made 97 appearances for Newport, 85 in the League. At the start of the 1974/75 season an expectant manager felt that, if a high degree of consistency could be obtained, promotion might be within the club's grasp. Brian strengthened his squad with the signing of the experienced Bobby Woodruff from Cardiff.

When I signed Bobby I knew he was a long-throw expert – he could comfortably reach the far post. However, he came in for pre-season training and said his back was killing him – we hadn't even started the season. There was an old speedway track running round the pitch where we warmed up. After a bit of training I threw the ball to Bobby and he didn't get it to the near post. A few days later someone from the League measured the pitch which was about ten feet too wide, so we got the groundsman to narrow it. Once that had been done I said to Bobby, who didn't know anything about it, 'Woody, far post.' 'I can't,' he replied. 'Just try it,' I shouted. He threw it halfway across the goal and I said to him, 'You've got a bad back, my arse!' I didn't dare tell him the truth until months after but it did the trick. I'd love to see him hurl one now, considering the weight of the old ball he used to throw – it would go from one side of the pitch to the other.

Promotion hopes were heightened after the first eight matches, which produced ten points and County were handily placed in sixth position. A big factor in their success was the form of striker Rod Jones, who hit five of County's eleven goals during that period. Twenty points from fourteen games up to the end of January lifted the side to third place and confirmed County as genuine promotion candidates. However the month of February proved disastrous, with injuries or suspensions to Peter Passey, Graham Coldrick, Bobby Woodruff, captain Brian Godfrey and Steve Aizlewood resulting in a slump in form. Two poor home defeats against Cambridge and Doncaster proved particularly frustrating for Brian, who was unable to field a settled side. A 3-1 home defeat to bottom of the table Workington forced Brian to give his players a last-chance ultimatum to improve in the semi-final of the Welsh Cup against Cardiff. The players responded positively to Brian's demands, but were beaten by the odd goal against the run of play.

On 15 March 1975 a 4-3 home defeat by Burnley prompted Brian's immediate resignation. The Newport board were informed of his decision by letter, and Brian felt it would be in the best interests of the club that he resigned forthwith to allow his successor as much time as possible to sort out the problems and draw up a retained list before the end of the season. The news was ostensibly reported as being a shock to the board, but Brian had already flagged up an offer to take over a pub in Chepstow, which would have given him greater job security. Whilst the club's form was a consideration in his decision to quit there was also discord behind the scenes, which proved a contributory factor.

The real reason I left Newport in the end was that I couldn't get on with the chairman, Cyril Rogers. The first nail in the coffin for me was when he turned down the transfer of Steve Aizlewood to Cardiff after I had agreed to take Don Murray, Gary Bell and £6,000 for him. I wanted to shuffle the side about and knew that Cardiff were interested in Steve. I had a word with them, as I played with Don and Gary and knew they could do a good job for me. The County board said they wanted Bell, Murray and £20,000 for Aizlewood. Rogers wouldn't have it when I said, 'Why can't we do a deal?' He replied, 'It's about getting two old lads from Cardiff – we can get £20,000 for Aizlewood,' whereas I knew the most we could get was £6,000. I said, 'If we can get them we can win the League.' Although I managed to get Gary he refused the package, and I thought if that was the sort of thing I was going to have to put up with, I might as well get out. By this time I'd realised that the only good chairman is an ex-chairman! He sold motor cars and knew nothing about football. I wouldn't tell him how to sell a motor car and I wondered who was running the club.

Having spent fifteen great years at Everton and five more at Cardiff, I also couldn't accept the attitude of certain players. After one home defeat all they wanted to know was how Wales had got on in a rugby international. When I see what Ron Atkinson, who was managing Oxford at the time and Jim Smith at Colchester achieved, perhaps I should have stayed on. We had one good player in particular Mark Aizlewood, Steve's younger brother, who I like to think helped his development – he went on to play for Luton and Wales. I'd had enough of the game at that point. If Everton had come in for me and offered me a coaching job I might have taken it, but as it was I drifted into various jobs outside the game.

The Newport directors were fulsome in their praise for Brian – 'We thank Mr Harris for what we believe was a tremendous effort on his part…No board could have expected any more from any manager…We would like to wish him the very best for the future in whatever profession he now takes up.'

11

Life After Football (Mainly)

I already knew a pub in Chepstow was looking for a manager, so when I left Newport I took over. I like to think my sense of humour helped attract the punters as mine host. There used to be an Army camp down by the bridge in Chepstow and soon after I started there about a dozen Army boys walked in. Prior to me taking over I didn't realise they had been banned as they couldn't get on with the previous landlord. They asked if they could come in. I said, 'Of course you can, it's a pub, isn't it?' I had a drink with them and then one of them asked if he could bring some of their mates in. About half an hour later about twenty walked in, but they were never any trouble. The locals didn't like it at first, I didn't know that, but the lads behaved themselves and mixed well with the regulars. Our kids used to stay up late and when the pub closed, if the locals had been feeding the fruit machine, they would put a few bob in and win the jackpot!

From the moment I arrived at Ninian Park to the day I left I kept my fingers crossed when the FA Cup draw was made that it would produce a Cardiff versus Everton clash. When it finally came in 1977 it was seven years too late for me, but I went to the match and left one of our lady staff in charge of the pub. After the game I met quite a few people and was late getting back. When I got back to the pub there were four coach loads of Everton supporters inside. I walked in and this poor woman behind the bar was overwhelmed, she'd never seen so many customers. The four coach drivers were all Liverpool supporters – they refused to go into the pub and got people to bring drinks out for them! The last person left at about 4.30 in the morning and, as Everton had won, it was a great night. When England played Wales in Cardiff, I was delighted that Kevin Keegan and 'Tosh' stopped at the pub on their way down from Liverpool for a couple of pints.

When I was there I started a pub team. One day I got my boots out to make up the numbers for a Forest of Dean League game as we were short. Two of the opposition went for me all the time and, with about five minutes to go when

1987 – Brian wins another golf tournament, this time at St Pierre, overseen by Dickie Davies.

we were winning 2-0, one of them went through me. I got up and whacked him, down he went and the referee sent me off. It was the only time I had ever been sent off and was also the last game I played.

I managed the pub until 1979 when Richie Morgan phoned up to ask me to be his assistant at Cardiff. The weather was dreadful during the winter of 1979/80 and the team were struggling badly. We decided the only way to give the club a half chance of staying in the Second Division was to get matches called off. It takes time to get players and we desperately needed new faces. I lined up a squad of lads with shovels and we took all the snow from the terraces and touchlines and piled it onto the pitch. We called in a referee and he had no choice but to grant a postponement. We were safe towards the end of that season with matches to spare and built a pretty good side that included players like Ronnie Moore from Tranmere, Colin Sullivan from Norwich, Billy Ronson and Gary Stevens.

I was only there for a couple of years. We went abroad to Majorca for a week at the end of the 1979/80 season. A new chairman had been appointed who knew nothing about the game and kept interfering. The previous chairman, Tony Clemo, had a yacht out there, which was moored up. One day we were on the deck when the new chairman said to me, 'Are you all right

1981 – Brian sporting his cup final medal.

for next season?' I replied, 'That's a long way away, I haven't even thought about it yet.' 'Well you should be.' 'Why?' 'Because we want to get promotion,' he came back. He came over to me and we had a contretemps which ended up with him disappearing overboard. Two blokes had to dive in and fish him out!

I knew my days were numbered from then. In October 1980 we played at Sheffield Wednesday where Jack Charlton was the manager and Maurice Setters his assistant. Of course they were right from my era. We lost 2-0 and Richie and I were having a drink in the boardroom when big Jack walked in. He said, 'Come and have a drink down here away from this lot,' so we went into the boot-room. We were going back by train, but had to wait two hours and Maurice, Jack and I put the world to rights with a bottle of scotch in about half an hour. It's something that as a player just wouldn't have happened during my time, so it was nice to mix socially with guys I used to play against. I knew the daggers were out for me, the chairman was a very envious guy, for example he didn't like the Cup final medal round my neck. The directors were with us when we got back on the train. I'd obviously had a few drinks, but the directors weren't impressed and a few words were exchanged. Soon after they decided I had to go – I'd had enough anyway.

I left football to become a financial consultant and in 1981 joined an insurance company in Cardiff, went through the training, but it wasn't me. I stuck at it for about four years before I left. While I was working there I was approached by Chepstow Town to ask if I could show them what to do in training etc. They were struggling in the League and I fancied the challenge. I thought I could help improve them, so coached and managed them and we got promoted to the Abacus League, which was my aim.

At the turn of the nineties I gained an introduction through an insurance contact to a new job canvassing for the Bristol evening paper. Then in 1993 I was asked by the Leeds paper if I would take over the canvas for the Evening Post, *which my son Ian and I both did. Then Ian became ill and had to leave, so my other son Mark took over and I then retired.*

I had done some scouting for Howard Kendall in the early nineties and previously kept in touch with Bobby Ferguson, who I met during my time at Cardiff. Bobby ended up as Bobby Robson's number two at Ipswich during their great days of the late 1970s and he asked me to work for them, which I really enjoyed. I would go and look at their future opponents to see what tactics they used etc. I would prepare reports and on match days brief the Ipswich lads on individual opposition players.

Bill Kenwright suggested now that I was retired I could do some scouting for Everton, so from September 2001 I have been covering the area around South Wales and the M4 corridor. I'm looking for young talent and there are some good young lads out there in the Nationwide League. It's great to be still involved in the game and I often come up against faces I know I played against. We try to recognise each other through the greying and thinning hair! I haven't changed as a person; I still like a joke and enjoy life.

Away from football, Brian's principal hobby has always been golf. As a member of Brackenwood Golf Club, he won numerous trophies in the fifties and early sixties. In 1961 he came second in the finals of the Professional Footballers' Golf Championship at Formby with a round of 85, three shots behind winner Ronnie Allen. It was the nearest he came to winning the overall competition. When winning the North West qualifying section he hit a gross score of 67, one short of the course amateur record. In the late sixties Wales became the first winners of the Ford Club Golfers home international title when they beat Ulster 8½ – 3½ at Royal Lytham. Brian played an influential role for the Welsh side, winning all six of his games. He was for many years a member of the famous St Pierre Golf Club, but now plays at local Chepstow courses.

I love playing golf, it's my favourite pastime and I used to enter the Professional Footballers' Golf Championship every year. My personal highlight was when I played for Wales off a four handicap. The criteria for playing for

Brian as mine host at the Cross Keys Inn, Tutshill, 1975. Father Harold is second left.

Wales were that you lived and played golf there. I've managed a hole-in-one four times and my best-ever round was at St Pierre Golf Club near Chepstow, which was a championship course, when I went round in 67. When I was transferred to Cardiff we moved to the city, but when I went to Newport we moved house to Chepstow. It could also have been because there are a few decent courses nearby as well! I play at Shire Newton now off a ten handicap; I don't play in competitions any more. I take Tom and Jerry, my poodles, out first thing in the morning and play nine holes to keep myself loose-ish. I stopped playing regularly in the early nineties when I started the job in Leeds.

When I was about seventeen I had a pushbike. One day the chain stuck, I bent down, put my hand in it and caught it in the chain, which badly damaged the fingers in my left hand. I couldn't grip with my left hand for a long time, so stopped playing cricket regularly and started playing golf. But I found I couldn't play left-handed as I couldn't grip the clubs properly, so I changed to my right hand. I played a lot at St Pierre, once with Nick Faldo in a pro-am tournament in the 1980s. I was on a four handicap at the time and hit some good shots. The last hole was a long par three, he was first to go and pulled it slightly off the green into a bunker. I hit a five wood straight as a die to within about fifteen feet from the flag. He chipped out of the bunker to six or seven feet, I got mine in two. We shook hands and I said, 'Thanks very much,' and he said, 'By the way, that's the worst grip I've ever seen in my life.' They were the only words he said to me all the way round, I was flabbergasted. I said, 'By the way, what did you get for the last hole, four or five, I know I got two?'

As a multi-talented teenager Brian enjoyed his cricket and at the age of sixteen hit a 'fine, undefeated knock' of 73 for Port Sunlight Seconds against Ainsdale Second XI. He scored his first century (102) against Sutton shortly after. When he joined Everton, Brian participated as wicketkeeper in the club's annual match against Bootle Cricket Club, organised and captained by Albert Dunlop.

I had a trial with Lancashire County Cricket Club when I was about sixteen, but nothing came of it. I didn't like the length of the game anyway; I haven't got the patience to play all day. Brian Statham was my hero and I used to enjoy playing for my local cricket team Port Sunlight. When I got a bit older I started playing for Stork, where I knew quite a few of the lads, but gave up cricket when I was eighteen.

I've also always liked my cars; my first one was a big Ford. I took my driving test at seventeen but had to wait until I was eighteen before I bought my first car. I've had a few Fords and also a BMW and Jaguar over the years.

12

Random Recollections
and a Fine Family

The match that generated most atmosphere for me was when we beat Liverpool 4-0 at Anfield! Seriously though there was a tremendous atmosphere when Cardiff played at Real Madrid and Hamburg. To play in Real Madrid was a great experience – how many Division Two sides had played at the Bernabeu before? We looked around the ground and it was awesome. I had a great time at Ninian Park and like to think I made a big impression while I was there. I took over as captain and what helped was how I carried on with my humour. That softened the process and our success took off from there. I used to do my fair amount of shouting on the pitch of course. Likewise, when I went to Newport they were struggling like hell in the bottom four of the Fourth Division. I went there as player-coach as Billy Lucas was still manager at the time. We started to improve and I think the light-hearted side of me helped the atmosphere and allowed the players to relax in the dressing room.

The nearest player to me that I see playing now is Ashley Cole at Arsenal. I can relate to the way he goes out wide, suddenly shoots past somebody with his pace and opens up the play. Tommy Smith was one of the hardest players I played against. We had a few ding-dongs on the pitch, but were mates off, and always had a drink after the game. I didn't really fear anyone on the pitch, with experience I got to know how to look after myself.

For me the Everton supporters were the most passionate I ever came across, although the Cardiff supporters were excellent, and also those at Newport. I got on well with the supporters at all three clubs. I was having a drink on the beach in Majorca on holiday once when someone came over to me and asked, 'Excuse me, did you used to play football?' 'Yes.' 'Did you used to play for Everton, it's Brian, isn't it? Have a drink; can I bring my son along?' We shook hands and his son said, 'Do you live in a big mansion like them other players?' I like to think that is a good example of the respect supporters had

Brian's son Mark with his two children Zach and Thea.

for me. I don't begrudge any modern player what he can earn from the game, that's life. What disappoints me is that so many current players don't even seem to be aware of the importance of derby matches. I am still a big Blue and get upset when I see fans walking away from matches with their heads down, because the players they have just paid to see don't care as much about the club as they do. It certainly wasn't like that when I played.

I've had various hairstyles over the years. When we went to America in 1956 Brian Labone and I had crew-cuts. My hair was bleached during the summer of 1958 when I wasn't with it. It happened when I was coaching at Butlins holiday camp and I think Wilf McGuinness was the culprit while I was asleep. I did get a shock when I woke up in the morning and the Everton players were flabbergasted when we had our pre-season team photos taken! Of course there was also the Beatles haircut in the sixties. I used to wear a waistcoat, I don't know why, but I liked to be considered fashionable. I started to smoke a pipe as I saw someone smoking one when we were playing abroad. He looked so relaxed, I thought: I fancy that, that looks good. I didn't smoke cigarettes, but smoked a pipe at Everton and for a while at Cardiff, before smoking cigars occasionally from a social point of view. I haven't played the piano for years – I had lessons when I was very young, but sport took over quite early. I also played tennis, virtually anything with a ball. We have been going on

Brian's son Ian with his three children Arran, Jordan and Jade.

holiday to Majorca for the last twenty-one years. I originally went there for a week with Cardiff City. It was there that I was in a bar where this bloke was pestering us with a monkey, taking these photographs. I said to one of the Cardiff lads, 'Start talking to him and I'll get the monkey pissed.' I fed him tots of whisky and after a while the monkey fell off this bloke's shoulder! I love Majorca, we have been all over the island, but for the last five years we have stayed in Palma Nova.

I didn't have any breaks when I was playing the game, my injuries were fairly minor. I've had a replacement right knee since I retired, so I have been very lucky. I put it down to when I played I was a bit quicker than the others. I was quite athletic which I put down to my father, who was always right behind me. He had a stop-watch and bought me running shoes with spikes. He would say eleven seconds was my average for 100 yards and always urged me to go under that time. It came off and helped me fly past my opponents.

We have two boys, Mark and Ian, who were born in 1962 and 1964. They were both good at football, but when we left England for Wales they only saw the oval-shaped ball. Mark does the newspaper canvassing and Beryl helps with the admin. Mark has two children, Thea, fourteen and Zach, who is ten. Ian had a kidney transplant in 1990, when Beryl donated a kidney – I was not compatible. We kept it under wraps for a while, but the hospital asked us

Still the best of mates; the two Brians, Labone and Harris, 1997.

2002 – Brian walks out at Goodison Park for the Centenary celebrations.

to publicise it so we could encourage families in similar positions to do likewise. Ian has two boys, Arran, six, Jordan, three and one girl Jade, who is sixteen.

Having been inducted into Everton's Hall of Fame, Brian enjoys meeting up with his former colleagues at the Gala Dinner held annually in Liverpool.

We are very happy living in Chepstow, but I miss the Liverpool area in a sense as a lot of my mates still live there. I still play golf there occasionally and enjoy it when I return. My career always presented challenges to me. At Goodison I was one of the few local boys in a team of stars, which is always a difficult position to be in. At Cardiff it was a challenge firstly to keep the side out of the Third Division. We also had to do well in the Cup-Winners' Cup to justify our inclusion in the competition. Then at Newport I inherited a side struggling to avoid being kicked out of the League. Through all this I have enjoyed the challenges and given them all my best shot.

The game has always been a religion in Liverpool. For too many years, as far as Evertonians are concerned, they have been the target in the pubs for the waspish humour of Liverpool's supporters. That same sense of anger, frustration, and determination goes all the way up the scale from public bar

Above: 2003 – Brian and Beryl in front of a painting of his most famous day in football – Wembley 1966.

Right: Brian's parents Ethel and Harold, photographed in 1986.

to boardroom. It is part of the football philosophy of both clubs that they never settle for second best. There are very encouraging signs that David Moyes is putting together a team that is starting to challenge the domination of Liverpool – it won't come a moment too soon!

When I started in the game a lot of old players talked about football in the thirties and forties and said that it was a better era. I thought it was just them seeing their past as better. I know that the influx of foreign players into the Premiership has produced some terrific players and the game has changed over the years. But there were so many great players around in the sixties. You faced up to marking Bobby Charlton or Denis Law one week and the next it was a derby match and Roger Hunt was there, and the following week it was Jimmy Greaves or George Best. These were truly great players and I don't think many people will argue with me when I say they would compare favourably with the players of today.

13

Tributes to Brian

CARDIFF CITY

CARDIFF and NEWPORT COUNTY

NEWPORT COUNTY

EVERTON

Billy Bingham

I joined Everton from Luton Town in 1960, I'd had a very good time there, scoring thirty-three goals and had just played in the FA Cup final. Everton bought me as they didn't have a right-winger at that time, although I felt that I was just going past my peak at twenty-nine/thirty. There were a lot of Scots in the team, but I was about the only Irishman. Brian was just establishing himself in the team which was not easy, as there were a lot of outside players coming in and a lot of opposition for places, but Brian soldiered on and made his mark. There were about three Liverpudlians in the team at the time, Brian at left midfield, Brian Labone at centre-back and Albert Dunlop in goal, then Johnny Morrissey came in. They held their position because they were good enough. Johnny Carey and Harry Catterick, supported by John Moores, were buying in younger players all the time and trying to improve the team, so they were under pressure and you had to play well to hold your place.

The America tour of 1961 was like a holiday for us. Other than on that trip, I was never sent off in my career. The game against Bangua in New York was broadcast live on TV. A black guy was pulling my shirt as I passed him, I stopped dead, swung round, hit him in the solar plexus and he went down. I went on the Johnny Carson Show that night, as they wanted to see this 5ft 7½in guy who had floored this guy who was 6ft, they showed me running in slow motion! Catterick fined me for being sent off, but I got my money back and Brian and the other lads had a great laugh.

Brian was a very fluid player and wasn't out of place in a very good side. He would get good tackles in and was very creative with the ball. He could change the play from the left side to the right side with an accurate diagonal ball or feed his winger on the left side, where he forged a good understanding with Johnny Morrissey. He became one of the fulcrums of the team and was influential in a lot of games.

There were plenty of opinions and strong personalities in the dressing room, but Brian more than held his own there. He was a lively and amusing character, he used to call me Paddy and he always had a good answer for you. I used to train with him; we did a lot of sprinting together. Brian was very pally with me, we were always close and I had a good rapport with him, we both had a sense of humour.

Kenny Birch

I first came across Brian when I was about fifteen. We were all amateurs at Everton and came through the junior team together. We both came from the

Wirral, although I played for Birkenhead Schoolboys. I went to Everton at the same time as Jimmy Harris, which was a year earlier than Brian, who was a good winger and ball-player, very aggressive.

When we toured America and Canada in 1956, we met different people on the QE2 including Stan Kenton of the big band fame, who was sitting in the dining room, and we had a jamming session from him in one of the lounges at night. I think we celebrated Brian's twenty-first birthday in the Officers' Merchant Navy Club in New York, it was our hide-out. We stayed at the Paramount Hotel on 42nd Street, just off Broadway. We were on the second floor and all the American kids who had just graduated at college were staying on the floor above us. There was a lot of noise from them and we were starting to get the blame for it. We came back one night and Brian said, 'I'll stop it.' He went up, knocked on the door, and whack! We got no more noise after that, but it probably didn't do much for Anglo-American relations!

There was a big bar down by the docks in Liverpool called Joe's Diner and all the crew from the big liners, which pulled in at Pier Nineteen, went there. We used to play them at darts and every third drink in their company was on the house. All the players went there for a few beers when we had a free night. It wasn't before the games; Peter Farrell was very strict about that.

We had a big bath of hot water at Bellefield we all used to get in after training, and on the left-hand side of the bathroom was quite a big plunge pool, about five feet deep, which was always full of ice-cold water. When you got out of the hot bath you had to go past the cold bath to the dressing room. On one occasion Graham Williams, who was in the cold plunge, threw icy water at anyone who went past him. Brian said, 'You do that to me and I'll...' Brian hated cold water, but Graham still gave him the treatment. Soon after Brian went back to the bathroom fully clothed and stood halfway round the door. Graham threw cold water at him again and soaked him. When Graham got out of the bath, he towelled himself and when he went to get dressed realised Brian had put his clothes on – they were soaked to the skin! Brian was a very popular lad and I've always got on well with him.

Wally Fielding

I was in the first team when Brian first broke through. He was a thoughtful player and when he was converted to wing-half, the change suited him well. At the time the turnover in footballers was terrific and Brian did well to establish himself in the side. He was always a happy lad with a big grin on his face.

We did get on well as we were always happy people and had a wonderful time together in America and Canada. Cliff Britton had gone, so we didn't have a 'Sergeant-Major' with us. Football brought us into a different world and we would have never seen America otherwise. We used to get £3 per day spending money and I was invited into first-class one day to get a haircut. I remember seeing Rita Hayworth there and the captain gave me a real dressing down for being in the wrong class of the ship.

I think Everton is the greatest club in football in the way they treat their old players. I'm the oldest surviving ex-Evertonian at eighty-three and they treat me like a lost child. Brian sits at the same table at me for the reunion dinners and always gives me a big hug!

Jimmy Gabriel

In the beginning the guys like me who came to the club in the early sixties didn't mix all that much with the local guys. Then Billy Bingham pointed out to me that I was young enough to mix with them and Brian and I seemed to pair up. We'd have a drink together and later on we were room-mates. The other new players started to mix well and it brought the side together.

It's true we had wine the night before the cup-ties on our way to Wembley but it was only a half-bottle, apart from the final, which was the big one, so we had a full bottle of wine. Sometimes you got more nervous in cup-ties than League fixtures because of the sudden death nature of the game. I wasn't a great wine drinker but it helped us get to sleep, and in midfield you needed a good night's sleep, as you were running for ninety minutes. I never liked to drink the day before a game, we never did it any other time, but we had to keep it going. I wouldn't recommend it, but the luck held and so did our superstition. I was superstitious anyway – I always put my left boot on first. We were playing 4-2-4 at that time, so my position in midfield was hard-going. Brian was playing along Brian Labone at the time and the workload on him was not quite so heavy. I wasn't really upset with Brian when we were 2-0 down in the final, we didn't have time for that as we got one back soon after.

Brian had more rounded skills than I did, he was a very talented footballer. While he could get up and down the pitch and score the odd goal as well, he was more of a player who played from the defence to midfield, then stayed there and dominated that part of the pitch. I was more attacking and tended to use the midfield as a start point and get up and down in a more forward role. Brian was a really good midfield player, but when he went alongside Brian Labone in a more defensive role during the latter part of his time at Everton, I thought he was brilliant. I don't know why Harry Catterick sold him, as Brian could have played for England alongside Labby were it not for Bobby Moore. He had great anticipation and you could see what a clever player he was in that position. Brian wasn't a big play-maker in midfield, he more changed the point of attack when he got the ball and consequently was underrated. He was a tidy player who got the ball and moved it around a bit like Colin Harvey, and did his job well. He didn't get on the end of things but never gave the ball away, used it effectively and held his position well. He could be flashy at times but he was a players' player, we really liked playing with him. Catterick wanted somebody else in there though and perhaps Tony Kay got noticed a bit more. I actually thought Kay might be taking my place. I was surprised when Brian went to Cardiff, as I think he could have played on at Everton for a number of years. He was funny without being offensive; he could take any situation and turn it into a laugh. When we played golf with him it was like playing with a professional, he was a natural sportsman.

Jimmy Harris
Brian and I first played together in the reserves for a few matches. I'd just done my National Service in Germany, so I hadn't seen much of him for a couple of years. We both made our debuts on the same day against Burnley and Harry Potts also stepped up from the reserves. I don't recall much of the game, but I remember an FA Cup tie at Port Vale (January 1956) when Brian played well and scored one of the goals in a 3-2 win. They were a good side then and we played in front of a big crowd. The conditions weren't brilliant and when we stepped out onto the pitch there was mud up to our ankles. The famous Spurs 10-4 defeat was my first hat-trick in senior football. We did slightly better in the second half, but they were a very good side and Albert (Dunlop) had a nightmare. It was in the days when centre-forwards thought nothing of barging into goalkeepers like Albert, who was not very big and Bobby Smith was quite intimidating.

Brian and I were completely different players, I was a centre-forward and played through the middle, he was a ball-playing winger, although we were both pretty pacy and direct players. We've known each other for fifty years now and meet up at the Everton reunions.

Colin Harvey
Brian was a very good reader of the game; his best position was playing alongside the centre-half. When Tony Kay went it gave Brian his best opportunity, as he held a regular position alongside Brian Labone and made the most of it. He could also play the ball out from the back very effectively.

He was one of the first to wish me all the best when I made my first-team debut in Milan and was always looking after the young players. I've got tremendous affection for Brian as, when I came into the side, he was one of the first to look after me and was a big help in my career. It wasn't until I was recently looking at the tape of the FA Cup final that I realised what a good game he had. Mike Trebilcock and Derek Temple got the accolades for the goals but, when you look at the game, we were under the cosh for most of the time and if it wasn't for Brian we probably would have got well beaten. He had a tremendous game and I would say he was our best player on the day. I wasn't a prolific goalscorer but, not only scoring the goal in the semi-final against Manchester United, but the fact that it got us to Wembley is one of the highlights of my career.

Brian was a larger-than-life character and played a role in everyone's development. He was a real mickey-taker, it was great for dressing room morale and, as youngsters we were a little in awe of him as we knew we would be the butt of his jokes. Even though he lived across the water Birkenhead way, he was definitely a scouser in terms of his humour. He used to give Roy Parnell and George Sharples a lift in his car and some of the tricks he got up to with them were unbelievable, like throwing their shoes out of the car in the tunnel. Then later when he moved he gave Brian Labone and Gordon West a lift and stories about them are legendary.

When I see him now at the Legends dinner with that grin on his face, it's like stepping back in time. He was a good footballer, has enjoyed life and still has that wicked sense of humour. He was a pleasure to play with and it's a pleasure to know the man.

Dave Hickson

Brian was in the forces when I first played with him in the first team. He was a good ball-player and as a winger was a great crosser of the ball, which was good for me. I always remember a game at Newcastle which we won 3-2 in October 1957. Brian and I both scored and it was a great win that day, especially as it was when we shared a room and we hadn't had much sleep! He was a great man for team spirit in the dressing room, but used to reserve his joking for the younger members of the team.

Tommy Jones

Brian was obviously a young lad when I was in the Everton side. I think what helped develop Brian after he started playing in the first team was when we went on the tour of America and Canada. The games weren't so strenuous and it was a good introduction to first-team football. I remember we had a party one evening on the tour and ran out of beer. Brian went over the road to the off-licence for more supplies and they wouldn't serve him as he looked too young, and he was well miffed! He had to get one of his older colleagues to go with him. He and Matt Woods got on very well as Matt was a similar age and they grew up in the reserves together. When we were in Canada Brian was talking to an electrician, which of course was Brian's trade. This chap said, 'Why don't you emigrate over here and make a career as an electrician?' Brian was seriously contemplating it as it was a well-paid job and I remember him talking to me about it. I said, 'Don't, you've got the potential to make a good footballer, come back to England, you can always go to Canada later in your life.' I'm pleased he took that decision, as he fulfilled his potential to have a good career in football.

He had quite an outgoing personality. We played a charity match at Goodison once and Stanley Matthews was supposed to play, but Brian was brought on to replace Stan as he was unavailable. Brian ran across the pitch to the right-wing and was trying to imitate Stanley with his pose – the spectators thought it was great. I was in the crowd behind one of the goals at Wembley in 1966, so remember well his contribution in that game. He had an excellent attitude towards football and a good personality, which showed itself on the field. I think you can read the personality of a player on the pitch and Brian was one of those guys who could play football and enjoy his game at the same time.

Johnny King

Brian started off as a wide player, which can often be an advantage to players like him who later on move back. Brian and I enjoyed for a short time playing together in the first team until I came out and Jimmy Gabriel came in. He played alongside me on the left-hand side of midfield and was very good at coming in behind people. I was the defensive midfield player, who picked up the second striker and Brian was given the freedom to get forward – it was a good combination. Having been a winger he had a flair for exciting people by getting forward and his strength was getting quality balls into the box. We played during a period that Everton were trying to get a decent side together, with three different managers, Britton, Buchan and Carey, who developed a very good team. It wasn't the best Everton side at the time, but it was a well-balanced team.

Brian was a bundle of fun, full of life. We did have a laugh after training, we always had a couple of hours together – it was a bit of fun and I was no different, I was out enjoying myself. I was only five feet seven inches and Brian was not much taller, but we felt like giants when Bobby Collins joined us, especially when Graham Williams, who was also a little fellow who played on the left-wing, was in the side. They would always come out of the tunnel first, as Bobby was captain and Graham always seemed to want to get in there behind him. The opposition must have thought we were a team of pygmies!

Brian Labone

Brian was playing very well when he heard rumours of Tony Kay coming from Sheffield Wednesday. After training on a Friday we used to come into town to the two little News Theatres in Liverpool, one called the Tatler. Being thick footballers we'd have a cup of coffee and watch the cartoons, just for something to do. We didn't really need another wing-half, but Brian had seen Harry that morning and asked him if it was true he was going to sign Tony. Harry was a very good manager, but always kept his cards close to his chest and said there was no truth in it at all. When we came out into the sunshine at about four o'clock after watching the cartoons, the early evening newspapers were there stating, 'Kay signs for Everton.' Brian was devastated, but fought back when Tony Kay was suspended.

Around Christmas we'd break a few rules and after a couple of beers we used to wander around town. I would be Brian's stooge alongside him, and people loved to ear-wig and interfere or try and help. We'd be about fifty yards away from Central Station and Brian would say to me, 'Excuse me sir I'm a stranger in your town, can you tell me where Central Station is?' I'd turn the opposite way and say, 'If you go along there two hundred yards, turn right, carry on, it's along there on the left-hand side,' giving him completely the wrong instructions. An innocent bystander listening would say, 'No, no, you're all wrong, I've lived in Liverpool all my life, that's Central Station over there!' We used to go to the Grotto at John Lewis' with Johnny King. Johnny was only a little fella and Brian would somehow get him to roll his trousers up and sit on Father Christmas' knee, it was really pathetic but a bit of harmless fun!

When we arrived for our tour of Australia in 1964 there were so many Everton ex-pats waiting to greet us, it was like landing at Liverpool Airport. They looked after us well and it was a marvellous tour. When we were in Sydney we went to Bondi beach – it was a lovely warm day and we went to a function where Brian took over the whole proceedings. He somehow commandeered the microphone and went down a bomb; he should have been an entertainer. On another occasion in Melbourne myself, Mick Meagan and Brian were in the wings watching a live performance of the Graham Kennedy Show, it was a bit like *Coronation Street* or *Neighbours*. Brian used to do a Freddie Frinton take, the old drunken comic wearing a battered top hat and singing 'Sugar in the Morning,' it was his speciality. Somehow Brian stuck his head through one of the windows at the back of the stage doing his Freddie Frinton act, with a broken cigarette in his mouth. I don't know how the cast kept their composure and carried on, as it obviously wasn't in the script! I still can't believe what the reaction was when I think about it now after all these years. How that must have looked to millions of Australian viewers I don't know, but that was Brian, a marvellous character.

Mick Meagan

Brian and I came up together through the third team and reserves in the early fifties when he was a winger. I was an inside forward but I didn't have any pace and was converted to a half-back. When we played a League match against West Brom, Brian – who was on the wing – moved back to wing-half when I got injured and I hobbled about on the wing, as it was before substitutes were introduced. He never looked back and had a great career at Everton.

If we had two matches in London on a Wednesday and Saturday, we would sometimes stay over in Brighton. Brian Labone, Derek Temple, myself and Brian Harris were walking along the seafront one evening and out of the darkness we saw this shadow running over the sea wall. We ran over to investigate and this young girl was in a distressed state. Brian had a few words with her, told her not to be silly and she calmed down. He did a good job and I honestly think that saved her life. It showed the caring side of his nature and was probably the only time I've ever seen him serious!

I played quite a bit of golf with him, but didn't take it seriously; I wasn't in the same league as Brian. We had a great tour of Australia and appeared on the *Dave Allen Show*. Dave put up these mini goal-posts and the lads were having shots at him, bombarding him from all over the place and Brian was in the thick of the action. There were silly things happening all the time, if you stayed overnight in a hotel, the bed would be somewhere else and you knew Brian had something to do with it! He was always a jolly chap; we grew up together with others like George Kirby, who is sadly no longer with us, Eddie Thomas and Kenny Rea. There was a great team spirit at Everton, irrespective of nationality or religion. Brian had a lovely side about him and we had a good time together, there was nobody following you around in those days. When I last saw him a couple of years ago I immediately recognised that impish grin, he hasn't changed at all.

Jimmy O'Neill

I played in goal when Brian made his debut for the first team at Burnley and it was soon obvious he had the potential to become a great player as a winger. In fact we used to say he was the best winger since Stanley Matthews. I played every game in America and Canada as I was the only 'keeper! Peter Farrell, who was captain, said one of Brian's games against Aberdeen on the tour was the greatest he had ever seen from a right-winger. He'd probably had a few drinks the night before! I was in the first team leading up to the 10-4 defeat of Spurs, which Brian played in, but fortunately missed that match as I had a cartilage operation in Dublin. My last game was the week before against Birmingham which we won, so Albert Dunlop stepped in for that one, otherwise I don't think we would have got beaten 10-4! Brian's a wonderful guy and I always look forward to seeing him at the club reunions.

Andy Rankin

Brian was a good player, very versatile and a very understated type of player, he made things look easy. He was very funny in the dressing room – it always stood out in my memory as I was very quiet myself. On one of our away games I was just getting ready for bed when I saw this shadowy figure standing in the hotel door-way. This silhouette had a trilby hat and a pipe, and it was Brian. Then I noticed he didn't happen to have anything else on! It was a bit odd as he was always fashion conscious and very well dressed, but you never knew what Brian would do next. On the Australia tour after some function and a few drinks Brian started doing his ventriloquist's dummy 'gottle of geer' impressions. I also remember from Australia he had a fear of flying – one flight we took off and fell a hundred feet. Brian went a bit pale and temporarily stopped his wisecracks!

Dennis Stevens

When I got to Goodison the first person I saw coming out of the main entrance was Brian. I asked him if he thought I would be all right there. He said I'd do well and I will always remember that. I had a good four/five years there and played a lot of golf with him. For me Brian was a very good player and I couldn't understand why Harry Catterick bought Tony Kay. Hooky was a great character and comedian, and good for the dressing room. We had quite a few laughs in the time I was there at Goodison.

Jimmy Tansey

My main memories of Brian centre around the tour in 1956, which was a big laugh and we had a great time. We were away for about six weeks, which was quite a long time in those days, with five or six days spent on the QE2. As a winger he had some good games, but I remember when I got an ankle injury Brian dropped back and never looked back – he was a revelation. Unlucky for me, lucky for him! Brian was good on and off the field, quite a character, and we had some great times together. He's one of the old Evertonians I would love to see more frequently.

Derek Temple

Brian and I both came through the system at Everton at around the same time, when he was a promising winger and I was playing centre-forward. There were a lot of good players coming through the 'A' team and reserves at the time, like Eddie Thomas, who didn't quite make it at Everton, but was successful elsewhere. A lot of them came from the Wirral, like Brian. He was tenacious, a good tackler, read the game well, wasn't bad at all in the air, and had good control and passing. He had all the attributes, so it was not surprising he went on to do so well. He was also very consistent and I can't remember him ever having a bad dip in form. When Tony Kay came, it looked as if Brian was going to be the fall guy but, because of his versatility, he came through that difficult time.

Looking back at the FA Cup run, I remember the first twenty minutes of the second replay at Molineux when Manchester City had a real go at us, but the two Brians and Westy weathered the storm, and had to play extremely well to hold out before we scored. For the final, Sheffield Wednesday played with a sweeper, Gerry Young. I'm not sure whether it was their usual system or because Vic Mobley was injured and they had to bring in Sam Ellis, who was less experienced. For the winning goal Colin Harvey hit a ball out of defence and I had wandered inside from the left wing. I just ran towards Gerry as he went to trap the ball just inside their half. As their last man, when I saw he slipped I was on to it and had a clear run on goal. Ron Springett hadn't come out too far so I couldn't chip him, not that I would have done anyway. I just saw the opening in the far corner and it went in. It wasn't an easy situation one on one, especially against a goalkeeper with Ron's experience, but I think the gods were smiling on me that day. If I had missed it I would never have been able to show my face again on Merseyside! I always say if it had been Alex Young he would probably have taken the ball up to Ron and dribbled past him. You're out there to score goals and at the time nobody knew how costly that mistake was, but later on I did feel sorry for Gerry.

Brian was obviously the joker, very funny, but I generally managed to escape his pranks. I remember hearing one day Brian dropped George Sharples off the wrong side of the tunnel and left him. George was such a nice lad he took Brian at face value as he pulled away.

Mike Trebilcock

The first time I really met Brian was when we were travelling down to Tottenham for my Everton debut on New Year's Day 1966. I was playing poker for ten shillings with Fred Pickering and one or two others. I got four kings and as I was the new boy there I said, 'Ok, I'll see you' and lost out to a running flush. Brian said to me, 'Would you like a cigarette?' I said, 'Yes,' but my hand was shaking so much I couldn't light it! The only difference at Tottenham between the spectators and me was that they paid to get in and I didn't. All the guys must have wondered what Harry had bought this guy for, as I had a shocker.

Then we played Aston Villa and I scored, but limped off with an old injury. I got treatment and came back just before the Manchester United game in the cup semi-final. The next week I played against Sunderland and was up against Jim Baxter. We lost 2-0 and I was left out of the side again. I had agreed with the reserve-team players to go down with them to watch the cup final. I thought that was great, as I had only been at Everton six months and had never been to Wembley. On the Thursday the team sheet went up and I was in the squad. I thought great, I'm going to watch the game from the bench. We were sitting in the lounge of the hotel on the Friday afternoon when the trainer said the boss wanted to see me. I wondered why and John Hurst said to me, 'You must be playing.' I replied, 'You must be kidding.' There was one place up for grabs as far as I was concerned, Sandy Brown or Tommy Wright at right-back. I thought they must have wanted me to go in and witness what Harry said to them. When I went in there was not only Tommy and Sandy, but also Fred Pickering. I still couldn't understand what was happening. Harry said, 'At times like this, there are decisions to be made and I have to make them. I'm leaving you out Sandy and putting Tommy in. I'm leaving you out Fred and putting Mike in.' I nearly fell off my seat!

I got a telegram from Malcolm Allison, my old boss at Plymouth, who I regard as my footballing father. It read, 'Just another game, don't worry about it.' Harry said the same. When we went in at half-time Harry still said, 'Don't worry, play your normal game and you'll be all right,' and fifteen minutes later we were 2-0 down. We thought Harry, being a Sheffield man, must have got a bet on them winning! I looked up at the scoreboard, 2-0, and looked at the other end to see Ron Springett, the England goalkeeper. I thought: They've dropped an England forward for me, looked up at the sky and said, 'Why me Lord?' Then I scored twice in fifteen minutes and he looked down on me and said, 'That's why!' I realised it was my day. Derek Temple headed down to me on the edge of the box for the first goal. Don Megson, their left-back came in to cover and I thought if I let it bounce he'll get it, so I hit it on the volley. Then we got a free-kick on the right-hand side and all the big boys came up. I was heading for the far post, where I knew the ball was going, but Brian said to me, 'Get out of it, you're too small for this!' So I stood on the edge of the box and thought when they challenge for it, I'm going to make a run for the penalty spot. Brian Labone headed it back across the box and, as I ran to the penalty spot, it dropped right in my stride and I half-volleyed it into the corner of the goal.

For me, Brian was the man of the match and he got me out of trouble. When we were 1-0 down I made a very bad back-pass to Westy and Brian was there to clear it up. It could have been very different for me at Wembley were it not for Brian.

Roy Vernon (quoted during the Australian tour in 1964)
A petrol millionaire had a magnificent pool overlooking Sydney Bay and, hardly had the thought crossed my mind who would be the first in, when I went in. I was sure Brian Harris was the culprit with an ill-disguised nudge. There I was in the pool, clothes and all, thirsting for revenge. Brian kept well out of my way for a long time, but he could not be on his guard all the time and I waited for the opportunity to even the scores. It came and in went Brian with a mighty splash and not as much as a word of sympathy from any of us!

Gordon West
When I went into the dressing room at Goodison to play my first game against Wolves in March 1962, I was almost paralysed with fright. I had signed from Blackpool on the Friday, nobody knew me and the cameras came in, I remember Wally Barnes being there. Brian called out, 'Where's your sun-tan, son?' But I kept a clean sheet and we won 4-0. Brian told me afterwards that although I had come from the seaside, my face was as white as chalk.

I didn't see Brian till the Monday, when he asked me for a game of snooker. I could play a bit, but kept missing the balls. I couldn't understand it, but Brian was wiping the chalk off my cue over my shoulder and the other lads were in fits of laughter. We went up the spiral staircase to a little restaurant in the old stand for something to eat and Brian said, 'I'll treat you to a steak.' When it came I got the salt pot and of course he'd loosened the top and the salt went all over my steak! I had no car so I had to get a lift from Brian with Brian Labone to the ground. He stopped the car just before the ground in sight of the floodlight pylons, leaned over me and asked this old lady, 'Excuse me, luv, where's Goodison Park?' 'There it is!' 'Thank you, dear.' Off we went, I kept quiet. The next day Brian said to me, 'Your turn.' You couldn't refuse to do what he wanted, so I said to an old man, 'Can you tell me where Goodison is?' Before the man could answer Brian leant across Labby and said out of the window, 'It's Gordon West, take no notice of him, he's just signed for us!' Unbelievable – this was all in my very first week. Fun, fun, fun, he was crazy in a nice way and was doing something all the time!

We used to get changed at Goodison Park and catch a coach to Bellefield, which was quite antiquated then. As we drove past some major roadworks three Liverpudlians were giving us stick. One especially cold day Brian got a bucket of cold water and as we came up to them he said to the driver, 'Slow down.' This fella was giving us his usual stick and Brian threw the bucket all over him! 'Tell your mates that,' he shouted as we passed them by.

You wouldn't believe the fun we had. I was just an eighteen-year-old son of a Yorkshire miner and Brian certainly taught me how to have a good time. I was only young when I married and when we got back from away matches in London it would be about 9.15. I would go straight home as I didn't want to get into trouble, while the rest of the lads all went out. They went on at me and I eventually relented, we had a few drinks and I was late back home. I thought of an excuse, said I missed the train and had to get the next one and got away with it. The next day I went with my wife to Brian's. 'Gordon had a good time last night, didn't he?' said Brian – enough said!

I went round their house once when Mark, their baby, was just eight months old. I sat down in the front room and Brian put Mark on the window ledge and pulled the curtains over him so you couldn't see he was holding him from behind. As a woman passed by Brian shouted out, 'Hello Missus!' The woman turned and replied with incredulity, 'Hello son,' and waved to the baby.

The stories about my nerves were a bit exaggerated, but his humour certainly helped me and, after Brian went, I took over from him as the joker. Obviously we would train hard and it would get serious when we came to Saturdays. I have a good photograph against Liverpool at Goodison showing how competitive Brian was. We were 2-1 up with the clock at twenty to five when Roger Hunt scored, and you can see Brian in the background shaking his fist at me. I remember when we signed Tony Kay Brian was heartbroken, but responded with a cracker of a game against Barnsley. I also remember him saying to me after the cup final, 'Westy you deserve a medal,' which was a typical gesture.

Ray Wilson

I actually played a couple of times against Brian at Huddersfield when he was on the right-wing. He was used more as a utility player in his early days and that type of player never seems to get the credit he deserves. Together with the fact that he was a local lad, it seems to me that he never really got the acclaim that he should have done. It's funny how spectators tend not to appreciate that sort of player compared with players the clubs spend money on. I think as a local lad he was taken for granted, which was a bit like me at Huddersfield. The Everton supporters looked at me differently as they paid a fee for me.

I enjoyed playing behind Brian at left-back, as I had a lot of contact with him on the same side of the park. He was a much better player than a lot of people give him credit for. He wasn't just a defensive wing-half, he was pretty adept at going forward, he had good vision and was also good at intercepting passes.

When the opposition were on the attack Brian was always the one who would read the game and intercept the passes. I used to wonder how he managed to read the game in the way he did. Generally players tend to wait but it was as if he knew where the ball was going to be passed. He could make opposition players look amateurish as it looked as if they had played the ball straight to Brian. There are valid comparisons with Bobby Moore. I was quick and relied on that to get me out of trouble; Bobby and Brian were very similar in the sense that they had this gift of vision to step in. They saw any danger a second or so before everybody else. You have to be gifted to be able to do that, I don't think it's something that can be taught. It's something you either have or haven't, then it depends on how well you use it and Brian used it ever so well. He was a good ball-player, again like Bobby Moore. He was pretty good when he went forward, I remember him scoring a couple of goals when he broke forward and just casually chipped the ball over the goalkeeper's head. I think his best position was a defender with the ability to get forward – he could mix it with anybody and had good ball control and vision in the attacking and defensive sense. We also got on very well off the pitch, we mixed socially for a couple of years and Brian was continually playing jokes.

Matt Woods

Brian and I were at Everton as kids in the early 1950s and came through the junior side together. I remember him as a fair player on the wing, which is a lost art today. We were good friends and had a great time together on the American trip in 1956. I played against Brian quite a few times when I went to Blackburn, then went to play in Australia, although Blackburn kept my registration. They weren't going to let me play to start off with, so I said I was going to pack it in. Two weeks before I got on the plane they agreed that, as I'd been such a good servant and didn't cost a lot, I could play – it was a game of bluff really. When Everton toured Australia in 1964, Jimmy Kelly, the old Blackpool player, was coaching the national side, which I played for. He came to Australia before me and had been down playing at Wollongong. He'd been over to England and for some reason felt we had a good chance of beating Everton. I was captain of New South Wales and we played Everton in their first match of the tour at the Sydney Cricket Ground. I played for a Jewish club called Hakoah and had a newspaper column. I wrote if they'd come for a holiday they'd beat us, but if they'd come to play seriously they'd murder us! I got some terrible stick but I was fully justified. There were one or two fair European players who had come out there, but at the time the national side couldn't compete with them. I hadn't spoken to Brian for about forty years, so it was great to talk to him recently about our time together.

Tommy Wright

I always found Brian a great help when I first came into the side. He was a player you could talk to and was very approachable. He was the old-fashioned defensive wing-half, a great passer of the ball, and one of those players who went about his job quietly and efficiently. He was vastly underrated and very consistent week in, week out and aspired to a certain level – Mr Reliable. I didn't find out I was playing in the cup final until very late. For me the waiting to know who would be playing was the hard part, but Brian being around helped calm my nerves. I thought Sandy Brown would play and Brian laughed and joked, 'I knew you would get the nod.' He probably said the same to Sandy!

We used to have a dinner at the Adelphi after the European games and it was always wise to check your pockets before you left, as you would find knives, forks, salt and pepper in them courtesy of Brian when you got home. I think he actually put some cutlery in John Moores' camel overcoat – he must have wondered what had happened when he got home. When we were at Blackpool for a game I remember two guys turned up at the hotel looking for him just as we were getting on the coach. Brian had offered to buy a load of washing machines and fridges from them the night before and they took him at face value!

Alex Young

I took to Brian as soon as I joined Everton and we became great friends. He was a very quick and consistent player, and a good tackler and passer of the ball. He was a good all-rounder, with no weaknesses in his game. I've seen him play at wing-half, full-back and remember him playing in the back four. He would play off the centre-half, almost like a sweeper. He was excellent at all these positions, Mr Consistent, and he must have been a good player to have been in the first team for that many years, when Everton were a force to be reckoned with.

We used to play golf a lot; it was a toss-up whether he was going to be a pro-footballer or pro-golfer. He was a great striker of the ball and a fantastic golfer. He certainly used to take money off me and I was always trying to get on his side of the four-ball.

He was a funny lad with a quick sense of humour and was always taking the mickey, especially out of reporters. He was a bright guy and I remember when we went down to London, if there were any pressmen on the coach, he would say as we went over the River Thames, 'That's the 'Thems.' These guys were always tricked into saying, 'Not the Thems, the Thames!' He would go to shake peoples' hand in the street, then walk straight past them and I can remember him standing outside Lime Street Station putting on a foreign accent and asking passers-by how to get to the station. We'd stand watching and used to howl when people couldn't tell him. Brian would also drive in his car past a bus stop with a big queue of people in the middle of Liverpool. He'd wave to someone and, as they were coming up to him, he'd drive away! But the biggest joke of all was when four or five players would get in a car, with Gordon West in the back. They'd pretend to be a squad car full of detectives trying to take Westy, a supposed dangerous criminal, to Walton Jail. When Brian would get out and ask passers-by the way, they'd stage a mock escape for Westy and wait for the reaction. There'd sometimes be a mad scramble, as the passers-by had a go trying to apprehend the run-away! He was a great guy to have in the dressing room when there was a terrific team spirit. There were some super characters in that team like Roy Vernon and Jimmy Gabriel, but the greatest character of them all was Brian, a genuinely nice man.

Harry Catterick (written in 1974)
I have known Brian for some twenty years and have always found him a cheerful and outward-looking personality. In my time as manager at Everton, Brian was an important member of our Championship and Cup-winning team. He was a player of considerable skill with great ability to use the ball, and he gave Everton great service after signing for them as a boy, his example on and off the field being of immense value to me in my managerial capacity. Although a local boy in an Everton team composed of many international players, Brian's popularity with the Goodison public was always evident, and at no time was he out-shone by the star players.

CARDIFF CITY

Gary Bell
When I first got into the first team on a regular basis in early 1967, Brian was playing centre-half on the left-hand side and I was playing left-back. His influence was immense on my career as he would talk me through the game. He would say, 'Push the winger wide,' or 'I'm covering, Gary.' He was a classic old-fashioned wing-half, a superb passer of the ball, a good header of the ball and an immaculate sweeper. When he broke forward he was as good as anybody. I remember one evening game against Sheffield Wednesday at Hillsborough when the winger went past me and crossed from the byline. Their centre-forward was six to eight yards out, it was just a tap-in and Brian appeared from nowhere with a perfectly timed tackle, whipped the ball off his foot and cleared the danger. He had a great sense of humour as well. We were in Zambia on an end of season tour of East Africa playing against the Zambian National

side. I knocked the ball out for a corner and was trotting back towards the near post, when Brian shouted over from about twenty yards away, 'You pick the coloured fella' up!' He had an immense impact not only on the pitch, but off it as well. He brought true professionalism from Everton and we fed off it. He read the game so well and in my opinion was the best signing Jimmy Scoular ever made.

Ronnie Bird

Whilst Brian was coming towards the end of his career when he came to Cardiff, he had a great spell here. Playing alongside Don Murray, it was like Bobby Moore coming into the side for me. He controlled everything from the back with all his experience and was magnificent. The respect he got from the players as captain was huge. There are no special games I remember, as he was influential in every game he played in. Off the pitch he was like Jimmy Tarbuck, playing jokes on everybody. When we went to away matches on the train we would play a game called 'Brunch' with cans of coke. We would always deliberately leave a seat vacant for somebody who hadn't played the game before. Brian would be moving these cans all over the place and someone would come and sit in that seat. Brian would say, 'Have you ever played this game before?' Whoever it was would obviously say 'No,' and Brian would get him to join in with us. We would move these cans all over the place and the new player would turn to have a go and moved the can. Brian would shake his head and say something like, 'Wrong move,' or 'You've played this before, that's the best move of the game.' We would burst out laughing and nobody ever caught on what Brian was trying to do!

Bobby Brown

I joined Cardiff the week before Brian and we lost 4-2 at home to Hull in my first game. I remember Brian said to me after the next game at Plymouth, 'What the hell have we done coming here?' I think we were 3-0 down before either of us had touched the ball, so when we first went there it was a struggle. We lost four of our first five games and it took a while to get going. I remember we beat Bristol City 5-1 on New Year's Eve and I scored twice, which was a turning point for me, I could see some potential there. There was quite a gap to close as we were struggling at the time, but we stayed up with a game to spare, which was quite an achievement. Then we started to develop from there into a good side, and the defence was put right with Brian and Don Murray, who benefited with his experience. Brian was a different class, he wasn't the quickest by this stage of his career but he knew the game and talked to people, who respected and responded to him. With his great experience he also brought the younger players on, giving them confidence.

He was a character who kept everyone bubbly. I remember being on the train on our way to a match at Hull halfway through our first season. Hooky was in a carriage sitting next to a seaman who had just come off a boat. He pretended to have a stammer and took the piss out of him for two hours. 'Who did you play for?' asked the seaman. 'L-l-l-liv-liv,' said Brian. 'Liverpool?' asked the seaman. 'Everton,' came back Brian! The lads were trying not to laugh as he had this guy speaking in a very loud voice as Brian was also pretending to be deaf. He asked Brian, 'How do you hear the whistle?' 'I look at the referee putting the whistle into his mouth,' said Brian! The guy then started talking about the manager, who was sitting close by. Hooky was saying all sorts of terrible things about him in a loud voice and the lads were all hiding behind papers and books.

He always liked a few glasses of wine before he played and would buy a bottle of wine as he couldn't sleep in strange hotels. He would set people up, saying something obvious like, 'Who is the Prime Minister?' You didn't know whether he was being serious or not, so I used to say nothing until I was convinced what he was saying was genuine, so anyone who didn't know him very well would dive in with both feet.

He was always very complimentary to me and I respected what he said. I wasn't the best player in the world because of my injuries, but he encouraged me and gave me confidence by talking to me and made you feel you were a better player than you really were – I respected him for that.

Dave Carver

When Brian joined us the position was pretty grim, we'd been beaten 7-1 at Wolves, were virtually bottom of the League and confidence was at an all-time low. It was such a surprise when he signed for us, as it was so soon after the cup final. You could see from the start Brian was a class act and he more than anybody pulled things round. His legs had gone a bit but he more than made up for it by the way he read the game. It would have been nice to have played with a younger Brian. For the two Hamburg games I had a little bit of luck as Graham Coldrick got injured a couple of games before, so I came back in the side. In Hamburg we went into the lead and it was backs to the wall for most of the game, but a combination of good defending and a bit of luck saw us through. For the second leg I still think Seeler was lucky with his goal at Cardiff.

Brian got away with murder and had a wicked sense of humour. When we played Rotherham, my old club, at Millmoor in Brian's first season, I was made captain for the day. As I ran onto the field I looked behind and nobody had joined me. Brian had stopped the rest of the side from following me out!

Brian Clark

When I first came to Cardiff I remember everybody had Vauxhall Vivas or Consuls in the car park, but Brian had a white Jaguar. I thought 'Hello, we've got a bit of a poser here!' Of course as I got to know him, I realised what a character he was. He knew how to look after himself, having been brought up in a hard school at Everton, and was an honest guy. A lot of people said I was the best signing Cardiff ever made, but everyone knew including myself it was really Brian – I just scored the goals. He wasn't very quick on the running track, but read things a bit like Bobby Moore, and had a quick brain and sharpness of mind that helped him on and off the pitch. We never tired of his stories – if something happened, he would say something witty and I would say to myself, why didn't I think of that! I think the Australian Football Federation are still paying for our trip in 1968. At one function where we were all lined up to be introduced to the dignitaries, a guy at the end with a big overcoat and a cap came along shaking our hands, and who was it but Brian, winking! He made a big impact in the European games, I sat in the stand watching him, as I hadn't been registered in time to play. Coming from Bristol City where we looked up to John Ayteo, it was similar with Brian at Cardiff. We were different characters but Brian was quick-witted and full of life and I had a lot of time for him – a top man.

Fred Davies

Although I played for Wolves at the time, I knew of Brian as my dad was an Evertonian, and so was I coming from Liverpool. He was one of those players who knew how to look after himself. He was very experienced and helped young Don Murray along.

He was such a character, with a dry sense of humour. When we were on tour I remember him giving a speech when Jimmy Scoular was sitting there. He said, 'Our manager is the only man who combs his hair with a sponge.' Only Brian could get away with that! He could knock them back but would always be the first one up next morning banging on your door. I remember on away trips to East Anglia, if you could get a seat on the train you were doing really well. Three of us were once in the restaurant car and Brian started a game (Brunch). We would use the salt and pepper pots, knives and forks etc. and he would say, 'Got you' when no-one understood the rules. A stranger sitting next to us was reading a magazine, when Brian said, 'Do you want a game?' The fella would pick up a salt cellar and Brian would shout 'Out' – we could hardly contain ourselves. It's a good job this fella was only on the train for an hour.

If the weather was bad we would go training on the beach at Barry. As we drove off Brian would say, 'I bet you I can get more people to wave than you can.' Sure enough he would wave and people would wave back. He got me at it and when this fella waved back at me, Brian stopped the car. I was screaming at him to drive on and this fella got to virtually touch the car when Brian moved on, much to my relief. There was never a dull moment when Brian was around!

Ian Gibson

Brian was a good player, he couldn't run as he was coming towards the end of his career, but he could read the game. He was very clever, nobody ever went round him as he always gave himself a couple of yards. In training one minute he was standing beside me and I thought I'd turn him, but he'd take the ball off me as he'd stepped back two or three yards, giving himself some space. He never got caught out – if he did he would obstruct the opposition. I only played with Brian for one season (1970/71), when we finished third in the League. Both Leicester and Sheffield United, who went up, were good sides and I think we did well to finish behind them.

I think we were robbed in Madrid in 1971 when we should have had a penalty. The bloke dived and handled the ball round a post. The ref said the goalkeeper saved it and gave a corner. It was a great atmosphere in the Bernabeu, and Madrid played Chelsea in the final, who knows what might have been. I was interviewed on the TV as they put a man on me and all he did was foul me all game. It was all sly, pulling my shirt, elbowing me etc.

Every Monday we would have five-a-sides, Jimmy Scoular wouldn't pick me, he would pick all the good trainers. The only time we used to try was against Scoular's team, we would try like the clappers and they liked to play till they won. In one game Peter Harrison the trainer was playing with us against Scoular, Peter kicked the ball out, I got onto it, did a one-two with him and we put it into the net. That put us in front and Scoular sacked Peter on the spot, we couldn't believe it! A training routine was to jump over somebody's back and do a somersault. Once Scoular went like the clappers towards young Nigel Rees, who didn't bend down quick enough and Scoular ran right up to him and fell over. We all started laughing and Scoular shouted, 'You're all getting the sack!'

Barrie Jones

I played for Plymouth against Brian in his first game for Cardiff when we gave them a bit of a thrashing. I must have been partly responsible for him wondering whether he had made the right decision, but we became really good mates. He read the game extremely well and I learnt a lot from him, like not giving the ball away cheaply. I enjoyed playing with him as we both liked to play football and, having won the ball, Brian's distribution was second to none. He never kicked the ball anywhere unless he had to, which is how I always wanted to play the game. He was steady and reliable and I think he impressed everyone he met. I cannot speak highly enough of him as a player and a person, and we respected each other's play. I know we did well in Europe, but we were desperately unlucky not to get out of that (Second) Division.

Monday mornings always started with a five-a-side match and Jimmy Scoular would always want to play as well. You always wanted to get on the same side as the manager, as it was a full training session, so more often than not Brian and I managed to get in his team. It would only last an hour, but if his side was losing it would go on till about two o'clock in the afternoon! When I went to Cardiff my first recollection was having a practice match for ninety minutes against the reserves, but the reserves were beating the first team 2-1, so it went on for hours until the first team won the game. Scoular was a hard man and training at Cardiff was tough, with long warm-ups, spins etc., we trained for hours. Brian, with his experience at Everton, and myself, having learnt under Malcolm Allison at Plymouth, suggested on a Friday morning we have a couple of spins, head tennis etc. and that would be it. We could then go for a nice bath etc. as some players were lasting the game longer on the Saturday than others. He didn't think much of the idea, then a couple of weeks later he would introduce it!

We had good trips abroad and the gaffer arranged fantastic hotels, which the players appreciated. We had a fabulous tour of Australia in 1968 and I put on about a stone in weight with all the drinking and eating for Wales, they looked after us so well. I remember after the game in Brisbane we went to a reception with all the officials etc. As captain it was Brian's responsibility to make the speech, but I don't think he knew what he was saying as he was so pissed – I laughed so much. We had a drinking committee on tour, Brian was chairman, I was treasurer and Ronnie Bird was secretary! They were great days and we had a superb team spirit which all successful sides need.

Peter King

I remember talking to Brian on the train after his first game for us at Plymouth, when we lost 7-1; he was wondering what on earth he had come to. It took a while for his influence to fully reap benefits, but he became a very dominant figure in the club and dressing room. He was made captain, but was injured at the same time as I was, and when he came back for some reason he didn't get the captaincy back. He was still looked upon as captain amongst the other players. He was very skilful for a defender, far more so than a lot of people gave him credit for. He was a tremendous comedian; the main thing was that he pretended to be deaf and dumb. Whenever we got into a conversation on the train to away matches with a member of the public, he would keep such a straight face. I remember one fellow thought Brian was taking the 'mick' out of him. Brian kept a straight face so well he was convinced, he was a natural. I remember standing in the foyer of a hotel once the night before a game and a chap started talking to me. Brian stood straight behind him and started pulling faces at me. This chap was asking about the game and I was trying to talk to him, and in the end I had to say to Brian, 'Brian, do you want anything?' Brian with a straight face said, 'No, why?!'

Richie Morgan

Brian was a brilliant man in many ways, on and off the pitch. My Cardiff debut in the Cup-Winners' Cup was one of those games you dream about, but without him alongside me it could have been an absolute disaster. We went out to Germany on the Monday and it was pretty obvious then that I was going to play. Brian had a great empathy towards how I was feeling, took me under his wing and calmed me. During the afternoon when some of the lads went to sleep, we sat for two hours and played cards, as he probably knew that the nerves could take over before long, in the build-up to the game. On the field he literally took over, he talked me through the game and told me when and when not to attack the ball. Being young and rather hot-headed there were one or two occasions where I could have lost my cool, but he said, 'I'll sort them out, you leave it to me.' His reading of the game and instructions were brilliant, he helped me so much. He was still a Premier League player playing in the First Division. Even after that when we played Hamburg and I was on the subs bench, he was immense. If anyone ever deserved to get to a European final, after his performances in the Moscow and Hamburg games, it was Brian. It was one of the great draws of coming to Cardiff at the time that we regularly had a back door into Europe. At the end of that season we went to Australia and New Zealand for six or seven weeks, and Brian was the ultimate ringmaster who showed the rest of us how to have a good time! Likewise, the year after when we toured Zambia, Tanzania and Mauritius, and had great fun.

I remember a guy got on the train at Birmingham for one of our trips up north and Brian played 'Brunch' with him for two hours. Fred Davies and I played and both got a kick as Brian asked this little guy if he wanted to play. He said, 'I don't think I've played it before.' As he got off at Crewe after playing around with these cans he said, 'Thank you for that game, it was most wonderful, I really appreciate it!'

When I asked Brian to join me as assistant at Cardiff his exact words were, 'Not if you just want me to be your ***ing sponge man!' I said I felt he had a few more qualities than that. Brian had a vast knowledge of the game and the input he gave me at that time was huge. We were fairly lucky in that we'd played five or six games after Brian joined, then had a bit of bad weather, it was almost like a mid-season break. It gave us a chance to travel round and watch a few players. I do remember travelling back from Cambridge just before the weather broke when we had been beaten 5-0. I felt there was no atmosphere and no camaraderie in the team. Being a competitor my first reaction was, let's give them a good bollocking but Brian said, 'Let's stop and have a pint on the way home.' He said if we buy them a few drinks, we may just call a meeting. We stopped at a pub then called a meeting in the back of the coach. It was like an open forum and I would never have thought of that.

You talk about Brian's ability to play and his tactical awareness, but from a managerial point of view he also had the ability to see what needed doing and blend people together. We went forward from there and had a really good season. Brian was very hands-on, I used to watch the game from the stand and Brian from the dug-out, and we generally agreed with what we were doing. However it's players that make managers, not managers that make players. Unfortunately Brian and I had our hands tied from a financial point of view and on many occasions we put a side out knowing that if the other side competed in terms of natural ability, they were going to beat us. It was to our credit, I think, that we could get players to perform out of their skins. It was a fabulous time for both of us, but in football everything comes to an end.

The knives had been out for Brian ever since the incident in Majorca. They waited for us to have a bad run, then the chairman said Brian was going. I said, 'If he goes, I go.' Perhaps Brian thought I'd let him down, but I couldn't afford to go from a financial point of view, so it was most unfortunate. We played at Sheffield Wednesday where Brian fell out with the chairman again and had another argument with him. Brian was such a straight guy; perhaps he should have been more tactful with the board sometimes and walk away from situations. It was difficult for me at the age of thirty, I would have handled things differently now. I'm not bitter, but am sad that I was put in an invidious position that I couldn't handle and I followed him about eighteen months later. Brian arrived just before Christmas, was with me all of the next season, and until halfway through the season after. In the first season we took them to the highest position – ninth – which Cardiff have never got anywhere near to since. A huge amount of the credit was attributable to Brian.

Don Murray

I have tremendous admiration for Brian, not only as a player but also as a person. He was a quality player, having just played in the cup final and was seen as someone with a pedigree who could bring so much to us. We had a lot of young players with potential and promised to become a useful Second Division side. With the experience and ability of Brian, it was a tremendous signing by Jimmy Scoular for the club and the impact when he came was almost immediate. Brian helped stabilise the team defensively and was a huge influence on and off the field. He made it so much easier for me, as he was a great talker of the game and this experience was invaluable for me. He read the game so well; if anything passed me he would pick it up. He fulfilled that role very well and playing with him gave me huge enjoyment and satisfaction.

As serious as he was on the field, he was full of fun off it. He had a typical scouser's sense of humour and was always pulling off different strokes. When we were playing a game in Brisbane on the Australia tour in 1968, at half-time he borrowed one of the bandsman's greatcoats and cap and walked out to the middle of the field wearing this gear to make a presentation! Back home he was into nailing players' shoes into the wooden floors of the old dressing room at Ninian Park. One of our players always wore a detachable collar to his shirt. Brian got hold of a smaller one once and swopped the collar. We watched as this lad tried to do his collar up and his face went almost purple in the end. Then all of a sudden you could hear this giggle from Brian!

Brian's contribution was enormous – Jimmy Scoular knew exactly what he was doing by bringing him in, and I think he was one of the best signings Cardiff City ever made. He must have been one of the best uncapped players of his time; how he didn't gain an England cap I really don't know.

John Toshack

When Jimmy Scoular, a tough, craggy old Scot, and a famous right-half from his Newcastle United days, signed Brian, we stood up and took notice. I was just seventeen or eighteen when he came and one of two or three local lads, and most of the other players were free transfers from other Second or Third Division clubs. We didn't have that many with First Division experience, so it really was for us a big signing, especially as he had just won the cup with Everton. We felt perhaps it was an indication of the ambition the club had. Hooky went straight into the back four alongside Don Murray, who won most balls in the air and was a very difficult centre-half to get the better of, and straightaway we could see his calming influence on the defence. He was a thoughtful player and became a key member of the side and a star, as Cardiff didn't sign players from bigger clubs.

We had the great European cup run and Brian was outstanding in those games, where his experience was invaluable for us. I think he relished the European games – they were probably for him a throw-back to his big days at Everton. He gave the side a confident air and that was probably where we noticed his value. Jimmy Scoular knew what we needed and what he bought him for and the confidence rubbed off on us. There were a lot of very good club players around at the time plus Bobby Moore, which prevented Brian from being capped.

I actually went on a coaching course with him when I was only eighteen years of age. The great John Charles also went for ten sessions on a Thursday evening. I think Brian always quite fancied me as a player. I can remember he gave me a few rollockings, but the impression I got was that he felt I could go on and do something in the game. When Brian was at the club, I turned down the opportunity of joining Bobby Robson at Fulham in 1968, then moved on to Liverpool in 1970. I remember Bill Shankly giving my wife a rollocking for wearing a blue coat when we first went to Liverpool, but I don't think Brian had anything to do with it. We might have been a bit naive, but we did know that Liverpool played in red and Everton blue!

In those days players just had one pair of boots, which we used to train in and play in on match days. When Brian came to Cardiff he looked around the boot-room and asked for two pairs of boots. I remember Jimmy Scoular saying to him, 'I only ever had one pair when I played.' Brian said, 'You can't compare the level you played at with the level I'm used to.' That was a player talking to a manager and in those days players didn't even speak to managers! Brian was pretty sure of himself but in a nice way. He brought a confidence, swagger and a great sense of humour that I was later able to acquire for myself when I went to Liverpool. He was also a great low handicap golfer; it must have been something to do with being brought up on those links courses. I remember he hit a very good three wood.

Bob Wilson

When Brian came to the club, as a goalkeeper it was different to what I was used to. John Charles was coming towards the end of his career, but he was an out-and-out centre-half. Brian played like a sweeper picking up behind Don Murray and I've never known a player to read a game like Brian. He seemed to know what people were going to do before they had decided themselves. He would just wait for the ball to come to him, he was so astute. He wasn't a workaholic, he wasn't the best trainer in the world, and would never run himself into the ground on the park, but you have to take into account the time of his career when he came to Cardiff. He wasn't a big bloke either but was head and shoulders above everybody else. Jimmy Scoular ranted and raved, but Brian as captain would have a quiet word in your ear. I can remember an incident in training when someone made a mistake. Jimmy cursed and swore, and Brian walked past and said, 'And that goes for your cat, too!' He was a role model and didn't expect anyone to do anything he couldn't do himself. In Europe he was head and shoulders above everybody else, he had a good attitude and was a calming influence. I only remember Brian losing his temper once – he would rather have a quiet word than finger point to get his message across.

When we were in Tashkent I remember Brian had a kick that opened a wound and he was given antibiotics. Within half an hour of the injection he was gagging and they had to give him a counter injection. I know I got good reports in the cup run, but for me all that goes by the board after the Hamburg game, which everybody remembers me for. I remember the Australian tour in 1968, which was our reward for doing so well in Europe. As club captain Brian gave the speeches, which were priceless!

Jimmy Scoular (written in 1974)

When I signed Brian in 1966 I knew having played against him when I was at Newcastle that he had the ability to get us out of trouble from near the foot of Division Two. We lost 7-1 in his first game and I can imagine what his feelings were because it was only four months since he had played in a cup-winning side, but I never had any doubts that I'd done the right thing in getting him to Cardiff. As the team captain he set a fine example with his steadying influence and consistency. In fact if he ever had a bad game I can't remember it for they were so rare. Every club needs a character in the side who can bring the best out of the others, and Brian was just that.

CARDIFF and NEWPORT COUNTY

Graham Coldrick

I came on as sub. for Brian's first game at Plymouth and switched from playing alongside Don Murray to right-back to accommodate him. It takes time for anyone to settle in, but you could see very early on that Brian was a good reader of the game and a good talker. I think he made Don a much better player by making him go for everything and sweeping up behind him. He was a good instigator of the game and I remember especially his performance in the Moscow Torpedo replay in Augsburg. I'd had a bad run of injuries and didn't play in the first two ties, but came back for the replay and thought Brian was outstanding in that match.

When I played for Wales Under-23s at Wrexham, myself and some of the boys went to a club at Birkenhead after the game and met a few lads there who knew Brian. We didn't know what his nickname was until they asked, 'How's Hooky?' It's a small world and we took that back to Cardiff with us. We had some laughs when he was about. When we went on tour to Australia and New Zealand for seven weeks, Brian ordered room service in a hotel once and asked for two boxes of cigars. He got them sent to someone else's room and signed in their name outside their room!

At Newport we held the record of about twenty-four games without a win and we really turned that round when Brian came. He was still a good player and a bargain, and people looked up to him for what he did, being an FA Cup-winner. As a coach he made training interesting, it was hard work but fun. A lot of coaches would run you ragged, but he brought variety to the training. We played in red, white and blue and he would set us the task of getting the colours together. It would take some thinking and Brian made it a good laugh.

When Brian became a manager, he had to distance himself a little and couldn't have a drink with us any longer after the game. He liked to try and play football instead of the long ball game a lot of teams played in the Fourth Division. We used to practice one-touch football a lot in training and keeping it on the floor, even though the players weren't as skilful as in the higher leagues. Brian would say, 'You've got the ball, they can't score, keep possession.' Overall he was a good motivator and a very fair manager.

Robert Summerhayes

Brian approached me to go to Newport the season before I went there, but I refused as I wanted to make it at Cardiff. Then the following year I was given a free transfer and joined Newport at the start of the 1972/73 season. I remember him as a hard player and a very good tackler when I played with him. I had three seasons there and really enjoyed my time, thanks to Brian. He was an excellent manager, always approachable, and very different in style from Jimmy Scoular.

Bobby Woodruff

I remember coming across Brian and Don Murray when I was playing for Crystal Palace against Cardiff – they were a bit of a mean pair and took no prisoners. When I signed for Cardiff in 1969 I didn't move house for about three months, so I'd have a few beers with Brian and the other lads on a Thursday. We weren't supposed to go out after a Wednesday, but we were doing so well no-one seemed to bother about it. I got to know him well and we became good friends. Brian was an excellent player, his distribution was good and he read the game so well, similar to Bobby Moore. Jimmy Scoular assembled a lot of good players like Ian Gibson and Leighton Phillips in my time there. When Frank O'Farrell was brought in halfway through the season as manager he dropped me. Frank bought Willie Carlin and John Farrington, players who had played for him before. I had played in every game that season, but never played another game for them. At the end of the season Brian was aware of the situation and I could have gone to Exeter as player-manager. I vowed I would never play at Newport, but I wasn't going anywhere at Cardiff and Brian persuaded me to move. He said he would give me a couple of 'grand'.

Brian gave me £500 when I got there and said I could have the rest in instalments, as the money came from the supporters club. Then Brian left and I ended up with another £500 and that was it. There was never any money at Newport – we had fish and chips on the way back from away games, it was very different from Cardiff. We had a different bus for every away game as we never had any money to pay the bills! Once we had only just got on the M5 when the coach filled up with smoke – not the best preparation for an away game.

It is true that Brian had the pitch narrowed to help my long throw, as I was struggling with my back. He didn't treat us any differently as a manager, he was very much a players' manager. There was a lot of respect from me and vice versa; he knew what I was capable of. If Brian had stayed at Newport I think we would have got promotion, but we had a very small squad and a couple of injuries made a lot of difference. One of Brian's biggest days out would have been when we drew Chelsea at Stamford Bridge in the cup, but he couldn't travel with us as one of his sons was ill. They had Charlie Cooke, Peter Osgood and John Hollins, a good side and we went 2-1 up and were playing really well. We ended up losing 4-2 but went back to the hotel and had a good party in the evening, Brian would have been proud of us.

NEWPORT COUNTY

Willie Brown

I was transferred from Carlisle a couple of years before Brian and the supporters club paid for my fee of about £1,500, as Newport didn't have any money at the time. Even though he was about thirty-five when he came to Newport he was still a wonderful player. We always thought of him as an understudy to the great Bobby Moore. He played and read the game the same way and we wondered what he was like at his peak. He was very calm and reliable in the way he played and I can't remember him having a bad game. He was a great mickey-taker – I remember when he first became manager we had many triallists along. He would get the crossword out before we trained and give it to the young, nervous, sheepish lads to complete. It was probably the last thing they wanted to do!

The higher level you play the easier it is to play the game on the floor, whereas it was more 'route one' in the Fourth Division. It was hard to play and manage a Fourth Division side as, if you started to play from the back, the players couldn't always hold it and pass it in the way you were used to, so you ended up mostly going for 'route one' and playing in the last third of the park. Brian was able to vary his game in the Fourth Division and players like him would have been able to adapt to the modern pace of the game, they were always one step ahead.

Wynne Hooper

I joined Newport from school, was an apprentice for a couple of years then turned full-time, so I was already there when Brian came. We'd struggled every year and were always applying for re-election, but Brian made a big difference. He brought a lot of professionalism to the club, which was needed, and we just missed out on promotion. As a player he was excellent with Steve Aizlewood as a central pairing and his coaching was spot-on. Brian was easy-going as a manager and he helped me immensely. I was a youngster coming through and Brian helped to build up my confidence and I became a better player for it.

He had a dry sense of humour, he would wind you up with a deadpan, straight face, and we would be easily taken in. He would never give anything away, then would start laughing. He was lots of fun and you couldn't be too serious with your football at that level. The last time I saw Brian I was playing for Merthyr at Barry in a cup game. I hadn't seen him for years and he came into the dressing room and gave me a big hug. I've got a lot of time and respect for Brian, he's a tremendous guy.

Roddy Jones

Brian was at the veteran stage when he came to the County, well into his thirties, but he displayed a coolness and calmness we weren't used to. He was able to put his foot on the ball and spray passes about, he wasn't very quick, but with his experience he didn't need to be. He had an excellent footballing brain and I admired him as a footballer. In his first game for us we lost 4-2 to Doncaster, who I think were managed by Maurice Setters, and it was a real culture shock for Brian. I remember him passing the ball, he put his right leg around the back of his left leg, flicked it and passed it out to the wing and people were looking agog at him as the ball went thirty yards right to the winger. No-one ever tried to do that in the Fourth Division!

I thought he was a good coach, he brought loads of new training ideas. I was managed by him for a season and a half and did well under him, playing centre-forward at the time and scoring quite regularly. I remember a game at the end of the 1971/72 season at Crewe which we won 2-1 and I scored both goals. I was a part-time professional and he said to me, 'You've got to turn full-time to further your career.' I scored quite a few goals and wasn't looking for a King's ransom, but County would never pay me the money I thought I warranted, so I stayed part-time. Brian stuck by me if I had a good or bad game, as I was always a 100 per center. We were fighting for promotion in the 1972/73 season when we played Alton in the FA Cup. Willie Brown and Lennie Hill had both missed penalties that season; we missed four or five on the trot and lost 1-0 at Peterborough the week before the Alton game, when Andy White missed a penalty which cost us the game. So even though Brian had scored twice in the Alton game, I said I'd have a go and scored. I think he wanted to find a penalty taker who could score from the spot. However, the next time we had a penalty I also missed!

I don't think Brian could ever understand the public of Newport, he felt they'd sooner go to bingo than support the County. He was dismayed at the lack of support when he left and I don't think the set-up was professional enough for him, bearing in mind where he had come from. I always got on well with him – he treated me fairly and I admired and liked him.

He would take the mickey out of everybody, particularly waitresses when we were having dinner. As they carried dinner plates to the lads, he would put his hands out with his palms almost touching their breasts as they walked by, then he would suddenly pull his hands back sharply and look at his watch. The girls must have thought that he was going to grab their boobs, but the number of times soup went flying was incredible as their natural reaction was to jump back out of the way! He would also talk to people and say outrageous things. They would utter, 'What did you say? I thought you said…' He would make it rhyme with something else he had thought of, then say, 'Oh no, I didn't say that,' whereas of course he had. Brian knew the lads were playing golf at St Pierre one day. One hole is parallel to the old A48 and it's got a long sweeping fairway. We all teed off and saw this bloke two hundred yards away run onto the fairway and pinch our balls. We all dropped our clubs and ran after him, and of course it was Hooky!

John Macey

Brian was a great player, he had skill, awareness and vision in being able to read the game two or three moves ahead. I was a sweeper-keeper, always coming off my line before Brian played and in a way we complemented each other, so I didn't have to come out of the box so much. He commanded respect at the club and liked his bit of fun but, once you started to play, he was very competitive. A lot of players learnt from him and he gave us a lift when he joined Newport. He set us up for the season which showed our potential, when we narrowly missed promotion. Brian and I went by car to Stockport to see the game which Aldershot drew to gain promotion.

I remember the game at Hereford when they first came into the League in 1972/73 in front of a crowd of 15,000, with spectators spilling over on to the pitch. Colin Addison was their manager and Ronnie Radford had gone from Newport to Hereford, so it was a real local derby. Willie Screen was playing at the back, with Brian sweeping. Willie went in twice to sort out their centre-forward Eric Redrobe, who was a big hard man, and came away with a knee injury, so he had to leave the pitch. It was the days of only one sub. and Steve Aizlewood came on and got done, he split his eye and Brian said, 'I'll sort the bastard out.' So he went in hell for leather and Eric did him as well. Brian had stud marks right from the knee-cap to his groin and he spent the rest of the game moaning at the referee, showing his leg and we lost 2-0.

Brian had this comic type of approach, like Bobby Woodruff, a very dry sense of humour. If you couldn't live with Brian's sense of humour it was hard, as there was no hiding place and the dressing room is a closed place. Woody would always pick the paper up, sit in the corner of the dressing room and come out with a quip. He was looking at the Stock Exchange prices once and, as we were sorting out our kit, he looked up and said, 'Ah, the balloon's gone up.' As quick as a flash Don Payne, our other 'keeper looked round and said, 'And the carrots have as well!' When Brian was manager we had a triallist down from the valleys. He was a big, tall, gangly lad and came with another youngster on a motorbike. We had a bit of a training session and ended up with a game of head tennis on the speedway track. Brian said to this lad, who wasn't too bright, 'You're not used to this game, son, these balls are hard,' so he made him wear his crash helmet!

Billy Lucas kept appearing on the scene in a caretaker-manager capacity. He was easy-going, very laid back and probably out of touch with the modern game by the time Brian progressed to manager. Billy used to travel down to the training ground for a little five-a-side after we had trained. We were practicing four different free-kick routines, like bending them round the wall etc. They were numbered one, two, three, four, but we never scored a goal in about forty-five minutes. Billy was kicking a ball in the background, getting fed up, as he wanted a game. He walked up to Brian and said, 'Brian, I'll show you a free-kick.' So, everybody stood back and Billy picked the ball up, put it down and toe-poked it straight into the top corner of the net. Everybody collapsed laughing and he said, 'There you are, Brian there's one, two, three, four and you can call that ****er move number five! Can we have a game now?'

Jeff Thomas

I remember Brian from his Cardiff European days, they were great nights and I watched all the matches at Ninian Park. None of us had his experience, which shone out, and for Brian to come to Newport was a massive boost to us. Whilst we weren't in awe of him, to have someone like that who had played in a cup final and Europe, there was a good deal of respect for him.

Brian came to a club that had suffered traumatic times and he brought a new dimension which took us to the verge of promotion. The year we nearly went up was when my knee injuries started. I got injured at Reading in September and didn't come back until the final half dozen games. I wasn't really fit but obviously as we were going for promotion they wanted me back. It was a bit silly really as I was having cortisone injections every week, half a pint of fluid was taken off on the Friday and I was just being put out to play on the Saturday. I couldn't go on like that as you had to be fit at that level and my knee couldn't stand the rigours of football, so I had to give up the professional game. Because of the injury I didn't do a lot of training under Brian, but he brought ideas in that no-one had seen before.

My biggest memory of Brian was being one of football's characters. He was such a bubbly individual with a dry sense of humour, a typical Liverpudlian humour. He was always up to mischief, always playing tricks, and was generally the life and soul of the club.

Andy White

Brian was a very good player even though he was getting towards the twilight of his career. His experience was unbelievable and what happened to the club after he arrived was all down to him. We had a good side and there was not a big change in the players, but in the way the club was run because of Brian. He was one of the best coaches I came across and made you want to train and play. We were playing football thanks to Brian and using the ball, rather than running about like a load of idiots. Perhaps it was because he had slowed up himself and didn't want to run! I remember him scoring with a header in the cup against Alton, I couldn't believe it. We were three or four up and I crossed the ball and remember him flying through the air to connect with it. I don't know where he came from or how long it took him to get there – it must have been one of those days where it took me a long time to get to the line, to give him a chance to get into the box!

Bill Lucas (written in 1974)

Consistency is the hallmark of any good player and that was a feature of Brian's game throughout his career. At Newport we were having a good run at the end of the 1970/71 season, but when Brian joined us that summer he added the experience which the younger players needed, and he helped them on the pitch in ways that weren't always apparent to spectators.

14

Career Statistics

Everton 1955-1966 – 358 appearances, 29 goals (in brackets)

Year	League	FA Cup	League Cup	Fairs Cup	European Cup	Other
1955/56	20 (2)	4 (1)	–	–	–	–
1956/57	3	–	–	–	–	–
1957/58	30 (6)	3	–	–	–	–
1958/59	35 (1)	1	–	–	–	–
1959/60	32 (1)	1	–	–	–	–
1960/61	30 (3)	1	5 (2)	–	–	–
1961/62	33 (1)	3	–	–	–	–
1962/63	24 (1)	1 (1)	–	2	–	–
1963/64	28 (3)	5 (2)	–	–	2	1
1964/65	31 (3)	1	–	2	–	–
1965/66	40 (2)	8	–	4(2)	–	–
1966/67	4	–	–	–	–	–

Cardiff City 1966-1971 – 202 appearances, 1 goal

Year	League	FA Cup	League Cup	Cup Winners' Cup	Welsh Cup
1966/67	28	4	–	–	5
1967/68	39	1	2	9 (1)	5
1968/69	17	–	1	1	3
1969/70	39	2	1	3	6
1970/71	26	2	1	5	2

Newport County 1971-1974 – 97 appearances, 2 goals

Year	League	FA Cup	League Cup	Welsh Cup
1971/72	38	1	1	3
1972/73	33	3 (2)	3	3
1973/74	9	–	2	1

Acknowledgements

I would like to take this opportunity to thank James Howarth at Tempus for agreeing to take on this publication. To Brian Labone, Mr Everton, the Toffeemen's last Corinthian and a marvellous man, for penning the foreword and Bill Kenwright for his rich contribution by way of the preface. To all Brian's ex-playing colleagues for their support and lively reminiscences. To my wife Linda for indulging me another sabbatical to enable me to complete this work. But above all to Brian Harris himself, a modest, generous and immensely likeable individual, his charming wife Beryl and their family, for allowing a unique insight into their lives to enable me to complete a thorough, open and honest critique of Brian.

Bibliography

Publications

Hodgson, Derek, *The Everton Story* (Arthur Barker Limited, 1985)
Platt, Mark, *The Essential History of Everton* (Headline Books, 2000)
Ponting, Ivan, *Everton Player by Player* (Guinness Publishing, 1992)

Newspapers

The Liverpool Daily Post and Echo
Western Daily Mail

Other Sources

Ambrosen, Tony, historian of *Newport County Football Club*
Everton Football Club
Gemini Photography, Liverpool
Mercury Press Agency Ltd
Shepherd, Richard, of Cardiff City Football Club

Selected Sports Titles
by Tempus Publishing

CRICKET

Lord's: The Cathedral of Cricket	Stephen Green	0 7524 2167 0

FOOTBALL

Aston Villa	Tony Matthews	0 7524 3123 4
Billy Steel: Scotland's Midfield Maestro	Bob MacAlinden	0 7524 2874 8
Bristol Rovers: Definitive History	Stephen Byrne & Mike Jay	0 7524 2717 2
Cards on the Table: Woking, The Conference Years	Clive Youlton	0 7524 2580 3
Cheltenham Town FC	Peter Matthews	0 7524 2730 X
Crewe Alexandra Greats	Harold Finch	0 7524 3088 2
Doncaster Rovers Greats	Peter Tuffrey	0 7524 2707 5
Everton: In the 1980s	Phil Thompson & Steve Hale	0 7524 2952 3
Home Park Voices	John Lloyd	0 7524 2949 3
Leed United Champions 1991/92	David Saffer	0 7524 3112 9
Leeds United's Rolls Royce: Paul Madely Story	David Saffer	0 7524 3071 8
Portsmouth FC 2002/03: Pompey's Rise to the Premiership	Richard Owen	0 7524 2935 3
Sheffield Wednesday	Nick Johnson	0 7524 2720 2
Tottenham Hotspur since 1953	Roy Brazier	0 7524 2924 8
Waiting for the Whistle	Andrew Waldon	0 7524 3055 6
West Brom 1953/54 (Season to Remember)	Tony Matthews	0 7524 3124 2
West Ham: Founded on Iron	Brian Belton	0 7524 2928 0
Willie Maley: Man who Made Celtic	David W. Potter	0 7524 2691 5
Wolves against the World	John Shipley	0 7524 2944 7
Workington FC	Nick Eade	0 7524 2818 7

RACING

Festival Gold: Cheltenham Gold Cup	Stewart Peters	0 7524 2817 9

RUGBY LEAGUE

Rugby League Hall of Fame	Robert Gate	0 7524 2693 1

SPEEDWAY

Speedway: Prewar Years	Robert Bamford	0 7524 2749 0
Speedway: Through the Lens of Mike Patrick	Mike Patrick	0 7524 2596 X
Wizard of Balance: Peter Craven Story	Brian Burford	0 7524 2856 X

www.tempus-publishing.com